Florentin J. Boudreaux

God our Father

Florentin J. Boudreaux

God our Father

ISBN/EAN: 9783741163845

Manufactured in Europe, USA, Canada, Australia, Japa

Cover: Foto ©Andreas Hilbeck / pixelio.de

Manufactured and distributed by brebook publishing software (www.brebook.com)

Florentin J. Boudreaux

God our Father

GOD OUR FATHER.

ROEHAMPTON:
PRINTED BY JAMES STANLEY.

GOD OUR FATHER.

BY

A Father of the Society of Jesus.

Author of 'The Happiness of Heaven."

"Thus therefore shall you pray : Our Father Who art in heaven."—St. Matt. vi. 9.

LONDON: BURNS AND OATES.

1878.

PREFACE.

IN presenting this little book to the public, the Author would express his grateful thanks for the very favourable manner in which *The Happiness of Heaven* was received. The little treatise now presented was the Author's first attempt at book writing; but circumstances did not then permit its publication. These no longer existing, he presents it to the same kind public, begging for it a share of the charitable indulgence extended to the other.

Though written principally to meet the wants of a certain class of pious people, it should not be inferred that they alone can derive profit from its perusal. Indeed, it is hoped that all, without exception, will be benefited by viewing God as their Father. Even the poor sinner, who has almost lost hope, will recover it and return to his Christian duties as soon as he becomes convinced that God is a Father, ready to receive him and to forgive all his sins. Should even one such be brought back to the bosom of our heavenly Father, the Author will feel himself abundantly rewarded for all his toil.

CONTENTS.

CHAPTER	PAGE
I. Why so many persons do not love God as they desire	1
II. If we would see God, by Faith, as he has revealed Himself to us, we must view Him as our Father	11
III. An objection answered	21
IV. We must view God as our Father, if we would be in perfect harmony with the New Law, which is one of Love	34
V. God is our Father because He is our Creator	46
VI. God is our Father because He has adopted us in Jesus Christ	59
VII. Viewing God as our Father is of the greatest help to us in the time of spiritual desolation	70
VIII. Viewing God as our Father produces peace of conscience as to our past sins	87
IX. Viewing God as our Father produces perfect love	100

GOD OUR FATHER.

CHAPTER I.

WHY SO MANY PERSONS DO NOT LOVE GOD AS THEY DESIRE.

MANY persons highly gifted, both by nature and grace, with religious dispositions, earnestly desire to love God above all things, with their whole heart, with their whole soul, with all their strength and with all their mind. In order to reach this perfection of love, they live a truly Christian life. They confess and receive Holy Communion as often as they are permitted; and they certainly endeavour to perform these two holy actions with the necessary dispositions. They hear Mass devoutly on Sundays, holy days, and even on week days. They listen attentively and respectfully to sermons; and they seldom, if ever, neglect the duty of prayer. In a word, they really try to be good, by performing all their duties, and by practising the virtues which their state and position in life demand. They are not only in earnest about saving their souls, but many of them are, moreover, aiming at a high degree of Christian perfection, either in the world or in religious communities. They are, therefore, members of that little flock which the Heart of Jesus loves so tenderly, and which He addresses in these words: "Fear not, little flock, for it hath pleased your Father to give you a kingdom."*

Now, we should naturally believe that, in all such persons, there exist a most tender love for God, a most intimate familiarity with Him, and a ceaseless longing to be united to Him for ever. We should expect to find "the peace of God, which surpasseth all understanding,"† reposing calm and supreme in the very depths of their souls. It would seem as if the thought of God, Whom they serve so faithfully, must be the sunshine of their lives, and that they already enjoy a foretaste of heaven. And so it is with many. They have every reason to believe that they are in a state of grace, and that God loves them in return for the love which they bear Him. They enjoy that peace which Jesus gave to His disciples, when He said: "Peace I leave with you, My peace I give unto you; not as the world giveth, do I give unto you, Let not your heart be troubled, nor let it be afraid."‡

But with others it is very different; indeed it is quite the reverse. For if we penetrate

* St. Luke xii. 32.   † Phil. iv. 7.   ‡ St. John xiv. 27.

beyond that beautiful exterior of piety which has led us to form such a judgment of them, we find, to our extreme astonishment, that instead of a tender and filial love for God, and a childlike confidence in Him, they have an inordinate fear, and even a positive dread of Him. They do not love God; at least so they imagine. Again and again have they endeavoured to love Him, but it seems to them every day more and more impossible. They see little or nothing amiable in Him, nothing that can captivate their hearts. They cannot even see that He is good. The fact is, they have to struggle much in order to keep the faith, and not to fall into downright infidelity. Hence, the thought of death, and of appearing before the Living God, produces in them impressions very similar to those felt by the condemned criminal, when he hears the prison door opened for the purpose of leading him to the scaffold. Oh, if they could only love God! If they could only believe that He loves them! How light their hearts would be, and what an exquisite happiness they would enjoy, even in this world.

This is certainly a bad state; or, at least, it has all the appearance of being such. I have not overdrawn the picture; for I have stated precisely what these good people feel, and what they say of themselves. In some, it is true, this depression of mind may not be so great; but in others, it even borders on insanity.

Before saying anything of the cause or causes which may bring about so undesirable a state of mind, or pointing out the remedies to be applied for its cure, these good people must be told, first of all, that, whatever they may feel or think of themselves, they most certainly love God, and that He as certainly loves them in return. Their love for Him is not sensible, it is true; but it is sincere and devoted. They do not, indeed, enjoy the sensible sweetness which God sometimes pours into the souls of His beloved children; but, how desirable soever such consolation may be, it is not, in the least, necessary to prove the existence of a true and sincere love for God. The evidence of a true love for God does not consist in sensible devotion, but in the keeping of His commandments. This is what Jesus Christ Himself tells us: "If you love Me, keep My commandments. . . . He that hath My commandments and keepeth them, he it is that loveth me. And he that loveth Me shall be loved by My Father; and I will love him, and will manifest Myself to him."* These clear and emphatic words of Our Blessed Lord make it as evident as the light of day, that the keeping of His commandments

* St. John xiv. 15.

is, by itself, a positive manifestation of our love for Him. Whatever, therefore, may be your opinion of yourself, and whatever may be your feeling, or absence of feeling, in the service of God, rest assured that you really love Him, and that He loves you, so long as you lead a good life—such a life as I have already described.

Nevertheless, it must also be acknowledged that such a disturbed state of the mind is not the normal or habitual one which God intended for His children. We shall, therefore, inquire into the causes which bring about this restlessness and apparent inability to love God.

There can be many causes whose combined action may spread gloom and despondency in the soul, and induce persons to believe that they do not enjoy the Divine favour. But we shall mention only three—probably the principal ones—and of these only one will be treated of at length in this book.

1. This total absence of sensible devotion, darkness and dread of God may be a just punishment which He inflicts upon us for our sins, especially sins against charity, so common among persons who make an open profession of piety. It may, also, be a punishment for lukewarmness in the service of God, dissipation of mind, idleness, a general want of generosity

toward God, and other imperfections; for God often withdraws all sensible sweetness in the practice of religion from those who are not generous toward Him. If, therefore, you stand guilty of the faults above mentioned, the simple remedy is evidently to take more care in avoiding sin, and to be more generous toward God.

2. This state may also be a trial from God, through which holy souls must pass in order to be cleansed from earthly stains, and be made to resemble Jesus Christ more perfectly. For, as St. Paul tells us, "Whom He foreknew He also predestined to be made conformable to the image of His Son."* Hence, after revealing to them His surpassing beauty, and filling them with the sweetest consolations, God, suddenly or gradually, withdraws from them His sensible presence, and then darkness overspreads the soul. All the beauty and other perfections which they had formerly seen in God, and which had so often been the subject of their contemplations, now seem entirely faded. Old passions, which they had so courageously mortified, and which they thought dead and buried for ever, suddenly spring into life again, and, aided by the devil, wage a fearful war against them. Their past sins and infidelities, which they had fondly hoped long

* Rom. vii. 29.

since forgiven and forgotten, rise up now in the most horrid shapes, and loudly call upon heaven for vengeance. In their unspeakable distress, they look up to heaven for help; but the heavens seem to be made of brass. They see there nothing but a thrice-holy God, Who seems angry with them, and on the point of hurling them to the deepest hell. This vision of an offended and angry Judge fills them with so great a fear and dread that their former tender love for God appears to have entirely died away They then feel, in a certain degree, the intense agony which overwhelmed the soul of Jesus when He cried out: "My God, My God, why hast Thou forsaken Me?"

These are some of the severe trials we read of in the lives of the saints. They are like a fire through which chosen souls pass in order to be purified from the remnants of earthly dross and imperfection. By such trials they are made worthy of God, according to the words of the Wise Man: "Afflicted in a few things, in many they shall be rewarded: because God hath tried them and found them worthy of Himself. As gold in the furnace, He hath proved them, and as a victim of a holocaust, He hath received them, and in time there shall be respect had to them."* Besides being purified and made to

* Wisdom iii.

resemble Jesus Christ the more, their merits are vastly increased; and, by such trials, they become more qualified to do great things for God's glory and for the salvation of souls.

Here, then, we have the second cause of that darkness of mind and dread of God. But, as is evident in the case of saints, it is a trial which comes and goes, and not the habitual path in which chosen souls walk; for after the fearful storm, the heavens brighten again, and we find the same souls basking once more in the sweet light of God's countenance. Besides, such severe trials are usually given only to the chosen few whom God conducts to Himself by extraordinary ways—ways to which none of us should ever aspire.

3. We now come to the third cause of the sad state complained of by so many professedly pious people, and it is the only one to which I call your special attention. You take wrong views of God. You view Him habitually and almost exclusively, as your Sovereign Lord and Judge, King, and Master, and almost entirely ignore His fatherly character. You forget that, while remaining your Lord and Judge, He is also your Father, and that He loves you infinitely more than earthly parents ever can love their children. You seem to forget that He is also your Redeemer, Who, having clothed Him-

self with our nature, exhibited His love for you by a life of humiliations and sufferings, and by a most ignominious death upon the Cross. In a word, you forget or ignore all that is most tender, amiable, and beautiful in God, and fix your mind morbidly upon those forbidding attributes, which, by their very nature, inspire fear and even dread. The natural consequence is, that you are filled with a fear of God so inordinate as to prevent you from loving Him with the filial love which He asks when He says: "My son give me thy heart."*

Now, what is the remedy to be applied for the cure of this morbid state of mind? The remedy evidently consists in viewing God rightly—that is, in all His Divine attributes, without ignoring any or exaggerating one beyond the others; it consists, moreover, in giving, in our minds, a bold prominence to those attributes which God has exercised more than others in our regard. In other words, it consists in viewing God habitually more in those attributes which inspire love and confidence, and less in those which inspire fear and dread.

It would be impossible, in so small a book, to dwell at length and separately upon the beauty of God, upon His goodness and unspeakable love for us, upon His mercy and

* Prov. xxiii. 26.

compassion for sinners, or upon whatever else is by its nature calculated to kindle in us a tender love for Him, and a childlike confidence in His mercy: yet we shall, in reality, do all this by viewing Him in the one Divine attribute, which is, so to speak, the origin or source of all His love and compassion for us—His Divine Paternity. We shall see, as we proceed, that God is our Father in a sense so profound that we can never fathom it with our present limited powers. We shall see that He has not only revealed Himself to us in that most endearing character, but, moreover, that it is His expressed will we should habitually view Him as our Father. Furthermore, we shall become convinced that, to consider God as our Father, is the source of peace, love, and numberless other blessings. For, as soon as this becomes your habitual view of Him, those dark clouds, of which you have so often complained, will disappear, as the morning mists vanish before the rising sun. A heavenly light will shine where darkness had brooded before; and instead of inordinate fear, there will spring up love, peaceful confidence, and a sweet familiarity with God. You will seem to yourself a new creature, gifted with the wings of the dove, wherewith to fly to the highest perfection, for you will then love God with your whole heart

CHAPTER II.

IF WE WOULD SEE GOD, BY FAITH, AS HE HAS REVEALED HIMSELF TO US, WE MUST VIEW HIM AS OUR FATHER.

WE cannot, in our present state of existence, see God as He is; but in our heavenly home we shall behold Him, face to face, in the unclouded vision of His Divine Essence. The glorious sight will fill us to overflowing with the most perfect knowledge of Him; and that knowledge, together with the ardent love which it kindles, will give birth to the happiness which mortal eye hath not seen, nor ear heard, nor heart of man ever been able to conceive. However, even in this world, we can know God in such a manner that our knowledge of Him will beget love and happiness, as perfect as can be hoped for in our present state of existence. But in order to effect a result so desirable, our idea of Him must accord with what He has been pleased to reveal of Himself. Our representation of Him must be one in which His fatherly character enters, not only as an essential element, but one, moreover, in which this character stands out boldly and prominently above all His other Divine attributes. It is true that the attributes of God, considered in themselves, are all equally infinite, that one is not greater than another; that He has no more power than wisdom, no more wisdom than holiness, no more holiness than justice. Greater and less are not in Him, but each perfection is simply infinite. Hence we have no right to exalt one of His attributes above the others when we consider them in themselves.

The case, however, is quite different when we consider these attributes relatively to ourselves; for it is very possible that, in our regard, God may have exercised one more than another; and if so, we may certainly exalt that one above all the rest. Now, has God ever done so in reality? Is there any one of His Divine attributes to which He has given this preference? Most undoubtedly there is. And which one is it? Is it His justice in punishing sin? Certainly not. For where should you now be, Christian reader, if God had dealt out to you His justice instead of His mercy? Should you now be reading these pages? Should you still be in this world, surrounded, as you are, with so many blessings, and having at hand so many means of reaching heaven? You certainly would not, if ever you had the misfortune of committing even one mortal sin. For if God had exercised

His justice rather than His mercy, you would now be doomed to exterior darkness, where there is weeping and gnashing of teeth. Truly, we may say with the Royal Prophet: " The Lord is gracious and merciful: patient and plenteous in mercy. The Lord is sweet to all: and His tender mercies are above all His works."*

This does not mean that His mercy is really greater than His other attributes; but it does mean that, in our regard, He has exercised His patience, mercy, goodness and love more than His justice in punishing our sins. Hence, in forming in our minds a picture of God, we not only may, but we must, give prominence to His fatherly character, otherwise we do not see Him as He has most certainly revealed Himself to us. This is an injustice to God, of which many good people render themselves guilty. In their meditations they picture Him to themselves, uniformly and habitually, in the light of a terrible Judge rather than in that of a tender Father. In their minds, He is an unbending, inexorable Judge, all-knowing, all-wise, all-powerful; having an unspeakable hatred for sin, and punishing it with an implacable and merciless justice. He is a Judge Who makes no allowance for the infirmity of our fallen nature; one Whose almost exclusive occupation is to

* Psalm cxliv.

watch His creatures with all scrutiny in order to find fault with them; one Who is never satisfied with their service; one Who is ever holding the scales of the sanctuary in one hand, and the rod of justice in the other; ever ready to strike, ever ready to pronounce the fatal sentence that is to hurl His ill-fated creatures into the "everlasting fire, which was prepared for the devil and his angels."

Here is a picture of God as painted by many pious persons who are earnestly trying to serve and love Him with their whole heart. In it we have only one attribute held in view, and that one exaggerated beyond all measure. It is an image of God in which the severity of His justice in punishing sin receives undue prominence; while His patience, in waiting for the return of the sinner; His mercy, in receiving him after his wanderings; the tenderness with which He presses him to His bosom; His unspeakable liberality in clothing him again with the robe of innocence, and restoring to him all the privileges he had lost by his many sins, are entirely ignored, or rather totally eclipsed. Who can have a tender heart and a filial love for God when He is so represented, or rather, misrepresented? This is not God, such as He has revealed Himself to us. This is not the ever-blessed and ever-beautiful, the ever-loving and forgiving God. This is not the vision of the Eternal Beauty and of the Eternal Truth. It is not our Father Who is in heaven. It is only a fancy, something of your own creation, which neither has, nor can have, any existence outside of your imagination. That this view is an injustice to God, becomes evident with a little reflection.

Let us suppose, for the sake of illustration, that you procure a book which purposes to be the life and character of St. Louis, King of France. As you read on, however, you find it to be scarcely any more than a catalogue of the punishments which he inflicted, with a severe yet impartial justice, upon murderers, rebels, blasphemers, and oppressors of the poor. These alone, in their most minute details, are dwelt upon, exaggerated, and painted in colours which fill the mind with horror, while his more winning qualities are ignored or barely mentioned. You had often heard that the charity of St. Louis was the most conspicuous of his virtues; that he served the poor at table with his own hands, and visited them in their hospitals; that he founded a great hospital for the blind, and that he placed in it, from the very first three hundred patients; that he likewise made provision for the poor, whom he maintained out of his own private purse; that he had every day one hundred and twenty indigent persons at table, near his palace; that he kept lists of gentlemen in reduced circumstances, and of widows in distress, in every province of his dominions, whom he regularly relieved; that he was merciful to all, even to those who revolted against his authority and attempted to fill the kingdom with bloodshed and ruin. These and innumerable other acts of charity to the poor, of kindness and clemency to evil-doers, are all ignored in this book, and the reader is left to infer that, during a long reign of forty years, the almost exclusive occupation of this saint was the punishing of delinquents and malefactors.

Who does not see the injustice that would be done to St. Louis by this very limited view of his character? Who would not censure the author of such a book for thus misrepresenting one of the noblest characters recorded in all history? For a view so partial does misrepresent him; not indeed by calumny and falsehood, but by an unjust silence, which leads you to judge that he was over severe and cruel, not to say bloodthirsty.

Now, this is precisely the injustice of which many good people render themselves guilty in reference to God. In forming their idea of Him, they look almost exclusively at the catalogue, recorded in Scripture, of dreadful punishments which He inflicted upon idolaters, transgressors of the law, natural or written, and other evil-doers, while they ignore the numberless favours which He bestowed upon them. By thus dwelling almost exclusively upon these chastisements, they evidently take a narrow-minded view of God, and thus unfortunately succeed in representing Him to themselves, to say the least, in a very unfavourable light; for in it His almost exclusive occupation is dealing out punishments to sinners. Now, if, as we have seen, the misrepresentations of St. Louis would be an injustice to him, who was only a man, what shall we say of the injustice done to the infinitely good and gracious God, by our perversely representing Him to ourselves almost exlusively as a severe Judge?

All that I ask of you is, that you take a fair and just view of God; that, by frequent meditation, you endeavour to picture Him to yourself in all His Divine attributes—ignoring none, exaggerating none, nor exalting one above the others, unless it be His love and mercy. This He has allowed and taught. You must, therefore, no longer let your mind dwell morbidly and almost exclusively on the terrible punishments which He inflicted upon evil-doers, especially among His own chosen people. You must also carefully take into account the wonderful favours which He bestowed upon them; the stupendous miracles He almost daily wrought in their behalf; the unspeakable love which He cherished for them, in spite of their revolting sins and base ingratitude; the numberless times He forgave them when they deserved chastisement; the unwearied patience with which He bore with them; the fatherly providence with which He supplied their wants and nursed their every care.

But this is not all. You are a Christian, and you must, therefore, appreciate favours which reveal God as our Father in a sense that the carnal minds of the Jews never dreamt of. You must, in picturing God to yourself, let the Incarnation of His only begotten Son have its place, as well as His life, Passion and ignominious death upon the Cross, together with all the graces of which that death is the source—faith, hope, charity, the sacraments, and other blessings which we, as Christians, enjoy. All these reveal His paternal love. "For God so loved the world as to give His only begotten Son; that whosoever believeth in Him may not perish, but may have life everlasting."*

Yes, Christian soul, this manifestation of God's love for us surpasses in grandeur and

* St. John iii. 16.

magnificence all other favours ever before granted to man. If David could say, long before the Redemption, that the tender mercies of God were above all His works, what shall we say now that He has delivered His own Son to death for our sake? When, therefore, in future you meditate on God, you must accustom yourself to view Him as a tender Father, since He has revealed Himself so prominently in that character. Unless you do so, you not only do Him an injustice, but, at the same time, you do yourself an injury; for filial feelings, familiarity and childlike confidence are impossible so long as you insist upon considering Him almost exclusively as your Judge. Your Judge most undoubtedly He is, but He is also your Father.

It was thus the saints looked upon God. Hence they could spend hours and days in the contemplation of His Divine beauty. Loving Him with almost seraphic love, and burning with a desire to see Him face to face, they exclaimed with the Royal Prophet: "As the hart panteth after the fountains of water, so my soul panteth after Thee, O God. My soul hath thirsted after the strong living God: when shall I come and appear before the face of God?"*

When they thus thirsted after God, think you

* Psalm xli.

that the severity of His justice in punishing sin was concealed from them? Think you they were blind to the lightnings, and deaf to the thunders of His justice? Far from it. But they saw this Divine attribute in harmony with the others, and instead of marring the beauty of their vision, it only made it more perfect. Wherefore, in spite of the thunders of His justice, they loved more than they feared, and called God their Father.

But you may say that nothwithstanding the truth of all that has been said, still the Holy Scriptures so abound with instances of God's severity in punishing sin, even venial sin, that it would seem as if He wished Himself to be considered as a severe Judge rather than as a Father. We shall, in the next chapter, endeavour to give a satisfactory answer to this apparently reasonable objection.

CHAPTER III.

AN OBJECTION ANSWERED.

THE objection we have to answer is this: When we consider the terrible punishments inflicted by the Almighty for both grievous and venial sins, would it not seem as if He did not wish to be viewed as our Father? This, I think, is the whole difficulty fairly stated. In order to answer it in a satisfactory manner, we will make a few observations, which, while aiding you to form a just estimate of the chastisements which God inflicted upon sinners under the Jewish dispensation, will also prepare the way to remove the difficulty in question.

In studying the life and character of some great king—the wars he waged, the punishments he inflicted upon malefactors, the rewards he bestowed upon those who signalized themselves in his service, his policy at home and abroad, and other things of the kind—we must be careful to consider him together with the times in which he lived. We must, moreover, take into account the prevailing religion, true or false, the traditions, manners and customs, as well as the peculiar character of his people. For if, instead of doing this, which is the plain dictate of common sense, we judge him and the events of his day according to our present standards, manners, usages, and prevailing opinions, we shall never form a fair estimate. We shall often be exposed to condemn where we should praise, and on the other hand, to applaud where we should condemn. This is a wise rule, which many forget while studying history; and hence, they never know history as it really is, even though they be well acquainted with its naked facts.

Now, if we desire to understand something of God and of His dealings with men, especially under the Jewish dispensation, we must carefully and constantly keep this important rule in view. We must have regard to the times, the circumstances, and especially must we take into account the peculiar character of the Jewish people. And what was their character? We find it graphically described upon almost every page of the Old Testament. They are represented as an ungrateful, gross, perverse, carnal-minded, stiff-necked people, upon whom the wonderful favours bestowed by the Almighty seem to have made no lasting impression. God was, therefore, constrained to give prominence to those attributes which inspire fear and dread, rather than to those which could have inspired the tenderest love in a people less carnal and and perverse.

Moreover, in all the punishments which God inflicted upon them, we must ever bear in mind the threefold end which He had in view. The first was to punish the sin itself. The second was to fill the minds of His people with a great fear, and even dread, of His irresistible power, and of His unflinching justice in punishing sin. This is what they are told in plain words by Moses : " For God has come to prove you, and that the dread of Him might be in you, and you should not sin."*

The third end which God had in view in all these visible punishments, needs a little explanation. The Jews had been chosen and separated from other nations, to fulfil a most important mission. They were to restore in the world the well nigh obliterated knowledge and worship of the true God. They were, moreover, to prepare the world for the coming of the Redeemer, Who, according to the flesh, was to be a lineal descendant of Abraham, Isaac, Jacob, David, and other patriarchs. Hence, whether they would or not, they had to remain one people. They could not be allowed to lose their nationality, by mingling with the idolatrous nations that surrounded them. Hence,

* Exodus xx. 20.

a law was given them, which, while it was a wonderful bond of union, also prefigured the New Law in its manifold rites, sacrifices and observances. That law was, in fact, the bud from which was to bloom the law of grace and love, bearing the more abundant fruits of salvation.

Now, if we consider the well-known character of the Jews, their perverseness, their proneness to idolatry, and their inclination to mingle by marriage with heathen nations, we shall see that the desired end could not have been obtained without terrible punishments, during the one thousand and four hundred years they were under the law. They would have been obliterated as a people, and would thus have frustrated the designs of God, but for the iron rod which kept them together, fulfilling their great mission even in spite of themselves.

But, besides the mission which they were thus compelled to fulfil among themselves, by preserving the worship of the true God, and preparing the world for the Redeemer, it was God's will to make use of them as missionaries, to publish His Name to the Gentiles, among whom scarce a trace of the primitive religion remained. Thus, while God punished them for their sins by making them captives and slaves to Gentile kings, they taught their idolatrous masters that there is but one true and mighty God. We shall give one instance out of the many:

When Daniel was thrown by Darius into the lions' den he was preserved from harm by the power of God. This stupendous miracle made so great an impression upon the mind of the idolatrous king that he immediately published the following edict: "Peace be multiplied unto you. It is decreed by me, that in all my empire and my kingdom, all men shall dread and fear the God of Daniel. For He is the living and eternal God for ever: and His kingdom shall not be destroyed, and His power shall be for ever. He is the deliverer and Saviour, doing signs and wonders in heaven and on earth: Who hath delivered Daniel out of the lions' den."* Here we see the different ends which God proposed to Himself in these punishments. The Jews are chastised for their sins, the fear of God is increased in their hearts, the world is gradually prepared for the Messiah, and the name of the true and only God is published among the Gentiles. Keeping these necessary observations in your mind, you are prepared to see these punishments in their proper light. We shall now give one striking instance of the Jewish perverseness, which made these awful punishments necessary. It

* Daniel vi.

reveals the whole character of that people, and their almost incredible hardness of heart, while it makes it evident that nothing but the rule of an iron rod could keep them to their duty, even for a short time.

Let us, for a moment, transport ourselves in spirit to Mount Sinai. Here we see a vast multitude of the children of Israel, "being about six hundred thousand men on foot, besides children and a mixed multitude without number."* They have just been delivered from a galling and degrading slavery by the most wonderful miracles, and are now encamped at the foot of the mountain, from whose summit they are about to receive the law from God Himself. I quote from the sacred text:

"And now the third day was come, and the morning appeared: and behold the thunders began to be heard, and the lightning to flash, and a very thick cloud to cover the mount, and the noise of the trumpet sounded exceeding loud: and the people that was in the camp feared. . . . And all Mount Sinai was in a smoke: because the Lord had come down upon it in fire, and the smoke arose from it as from a furnace: and all the mount was terrible. And the Lord spoke all these words: 'I am the Lord thy God, who brought thee out of the land

* Exodus xii. 37.

of Egypt, out of the house of bondage. Thou shalt not have strange gods before Me.'"*

Certainly this is one of the grandest and most sublime scenes ever witnessed in this world; and one would think it should have made so deep and lasting an impression upon the Jewish people that they never could have even thought of worshipping false gods. For, "being terrified and struck with great fear, they stood afar off, saying to Moses: Speak thou to us, and we will hear: let not the Lord speak to us, lest we die."†

Nevertheless, see what happens almost immediately after. The echoes of the thunders have scarcely died away in the distance; the voice of God is yet ringing in their ears; Moses is in the cloud which still covers the mountain, conversing with God, and yet they shamefully fall into idolatry. Listen again to the sacred text:

"And the people seeing that Moses delayed to come down from the mount, gathering together against Aaron, said: Arise, make us gods, that may go before us: for as to this Moses, the man that brought us out of the land of Egypt, we know not what has befallen him. And Aaron said to them, take the golden earrings from the ears of your wives, and your sons

---

* Exodus xix., xx.   † *Ibid.* xx.

and daughters, and bring them to me. And the people did what he had commanded, bringing the ear-rings to Aaron. And when he had received them he fashioned them by the founder's work, and made of them a molten calf. And they said: these are thy gods, O Israel, that have brought thee out of thee land of Egypt."*

Now, when, under all these circumstances we behold that immense multitude prostrate before this abominable idol, and worshipping it with holocausts and peace-offerings, what are we to expect? Nothing, of course, except the terrible punishment which fell upon them that very day. "And there were slain that day about three and twenty thousand men."† This certainly is terrible beyond the power of words to express. It actually chills our blood, and yet nothing but such a punishment could open their eyes, and bring them back to their duty.

If this whole occurrence were not related in Holy Scripture, we could never believe that a people who had witnessed the grand scene already described, and heard the solemn voice of God forbidding idolatry, could have remained so blind and perverse. And mark it well, this is far from being the only instance of their falling into that sin. Idolatry was one of their

* Exodus xxxii.   † *Ibid.*

besetting crimes; and one, too, not unfrequently accompanied by sins against nature so abominable that the mere recital of them fills our minds with horror. Here is a summary of Jewish history, taken from the one hundred and fifth psalm.

"And they mingled among the heathens, and learned their works: and served their idols, and it became a stumbling block to them. And they sacrificed their sons and their daughters to devils. And they shed innocent blood: the blood of their sons, and of their daughters, which they sacrificed to the idols of Chanaan. And the land was polluted with blood, and was defiled with their works. . . . And the Lord was exceedingly angry with His people: and He abhorred His inheritance. And He delivered them into the hands of the nations: and they that hated them had dominion over them. And their enemies afflicted them: and they were humbled under their hands. Many times He delivered them. . . . And He saw when they were in tribulation: and He heard their prayer. . . . And he gave them unto mercies in the sight of all those that had made them captives."

Here we have the substance of Jewish history, the repeated falls into idolatry, unnatural, shameful and nameless sins. These are followed by punishments the most fearful, such as war, captivity, pestilence and starvation. Then the people repenting, and turning away from their false gods and evil ways, call upon Heaven for mercy. Their prayer is heard; they are again and again even miraculously delivered from the evils brought on by their sins. In a short time, however, we see them again falling into their abominations. Evidently such a people could not be led by love. Fear alone seems to have made any impression upon their carnal minds; and, even, in spite of that, they sinned and continued sinning until their crimes culminated in rejecting and crucifying their God and our God—the Lord Jesus Christ. This last deed seems to have filled the measure of their sins; for they were cast off as a people, and scattered among the nations of the earth. Here then we have the reason why, under the Jewish dispensation, God gave such prominence to His sterner attributes of severity, power, majesty, and whatever else could fill the mind with deepest reverence, fear, and even dread, rather than to those more amiable attributes so capable of exciting love in hearts where love is to be found. The Jewish people, it seems, could not learn to love, and hence they were taught to fear.

This necessary fear of God being, as is evident,

one of the grand objects which God had in view in the old dispensation, it becomes easy both to understand and explain what might otherwise appear altogether inexplicable; I mean the terrific punishments inflicted, at times, for venial sins. Let us take one single instance out of the many—the sudden death of Oza for touching the swaying Ark. It does not appear that he was guilty of any great irreverence; he certainly meant none; but fearing that the Ark might fall, he stretched forth his hand intending to stay it, and yet, in the presence of the multitude, he was struck dead on the very spot.

Now, from all that has hitherto been said, and from the whole tenor and spirit of the Old Law, it is plain that this severe visitation was not so much to punish the rashness of Oza, as to inspire the Jews with an exceeding reverence and fear for the holy Ark of the living God. Moreover, He Who gave us life can, at any moment, take it away without doing us any injustice. Besides, we are not obliged to believe that this visible punishment was followed by any other beyond the grave. On the contrary, we may rest assured that if Oza had no other sin to account for, he is saved, and that, consequently, no real harm befell him. It may even have been the greatest mercy ever bestowed upon him. But, however that may be, it is very certain that by this visible punishment was obtained the grand object which God had in view—namely, an increased fear in the hearts of His people, and an unbounded reverence for the Ark which contained the law, and which was the sanctuary whence He spoke. Therefore, this and other manifestations of God's severity in punishing even venial sins, harmonize perfectly with the existing circumstances, the peculiar character of the Jewish people, and the end which was to be attained.

From all this, we see that the Jews, as a people, did not habitually view the great God in the light of a Father. He revealed Himself to them, from the first, as a most tender Father, Whose compassion for His afflicted children led Him to deliver them from the degrading slavery under which they had so long groaned and suffered. To effect this He wrought with outstretched arm the grandest of miracles in their behalf. Soon, however, compelled by their idolatry, their repeated rebellions, and their endless murmurings, He gave a bold prominence to His sterner attributes, so that they as a people saw in Him afterward only the mighty Sovereign, the King of kings, the Lord of lords, the great Jehovah, whose holiness, power, majesty, and severity in punishing sin, filled their minds with awe and dread. Hence, they endearing name of Father. They spoke to Him as to their Lord and Master, the great and mighty God, the terrible God, the thrice-holy God; but to speak to Him familiarly as we do, and say: "Our Father Who art in Heaven," seems never to have entered their minds.

In all I have said, however, I do not mean to assert that, under the Jewish dispensation, no one loved God or served Him with fidelity; for it is well known that there were, in those days, many saintly persons who loved and served Him so faithfully that they may be held up as models in any age of Christianity. Much less do I mean to insinuate that the Jews had not a very high idea of God's infinite goodness and mercy; for they undoubtedly had, and an unbounded confidence, too, in that mercy when they turned away from their evil ways, and returned to God with their whole heart. Never, perhaps, did a people place such confidence in the goodness of God, and never did a people experience more striking manifestations of His mercy in forgiving and forgetting the past. But I repeat that for reasons already given, the fear of God had a prominence in the Old Law, which, by His express will, it has not in the New. For the New Law under which we have the happiness of living, not only permits, but even commands, us to look up confidently, and say: "Our Father Who art in Heaven."

CHAPTER IV.

WE MUST VIEW GOD AS OUR FATHER, IF WE WOULD BE IN PERFECT HARMONY WITH THE NEW LAW, WHICH IS ONE OF LOVE.

HAVING seen, in the preceding chapter, that the Old Law was one of fear, and that this feature was in perfect harmony with the then existing circumstances, the ends to be attained, and the peculiar character of the people to whom the law was given, we shall now dwell for a few moments upon the spirit of the New Law, which is one of love. And here we shall see that to speak to God, and of God, as our Father, is in perfect harmony with the Christian dispensation.

The Jewish law was given from the summit of a mountain amidst lightnings and thunders, fire and smoke, the sound of the trumpet, and whatever else could fill the mind of the Jews with fear and wonder. Not so with the New Law. All, on the contrary, is here calculated to drive away fear, and to inspire confidence and love. When the fulness of time was come, the eternal Son of God made His appearance in our frail nature and promulgated the law of grace and love. "And seeing the multitude,

He went up into a mountain, and when He was sat down His disciples came unto Him. And opening His mouth He taught them."* But no dark cloud covers the mountain; no deafening thunders are heard; no angry flashes of lightning terrify the multitude. There is nothing forbidding either in His voice, words, or appearance. We see, on the contrary, in His whole exterior, a certain indescribable something, so sweet, so humble, so meek and captivating that the people are filled with admiration and love. They do not, as their fathers had done at the foot of Mount Sinai, beg Him to speak no longer, lest they should die; on the contrary, they follow Him whithersoever He goes in order to hear more and more of His life-giving doctrine.

But the remarkable feature of His very first sermon on the Mount is the fact that our blessed Lord constantly calls God our Father. Mark this well, listen to Him attentively, and ponder upon His words. How beautifully they reveal the spirit of that New Law—that law of love—which He is come to promulgate! "Take heed that you do not your justice before men, to be seen by them: otherwise you will not have a reward of your Father Who is in Heaven. . . . Pray for them that persecute and calum-

* St. Matt. v. 1.

niate you, that you may be the children of your Father Who is in Heaven, Who maketh His sun to rise upon the good and the bad, and raineth upon the just and the unjust. . . Behold the birds of the air, for they neither sow, nor do they reap, nor gather into barns: and your heavenly Father feedeth them. . . . If you, then, being evil, know how to give good gifts to your children; how much more will your Father Who is in Heaven give good things to them that ask Him, . . . For if you will forgive men their offences, your heavenly Father will forgive you also your offences. But if you will not forgive men, neither will your Father forgive your offences. . . . Thus, therefore shall you pray: Our Father Who art in Heaven. . . . Be ye, therefore, perfect, as also your heavenly Father is perfect."

From these and many other similar expressions found in the very first sermon which Jesus Christ ever preached, it is evidently the expressed will of God that we Christians should view Him as our Father. What a sweet consolation there is in this new manifestation of God's love for us! Can we not exclaim with far more reason than David that the tender mercies of God are above all His other works? Yes, Christian soul, the great Jehovah, the mighty, the terrible God of the Jews, hides from your gaze the dazzling splendours of His majesty and power, and gives prominence only to the attributes of His paternity—"Of Whom all paternity in heaven and earth is named."* He desires that, in future, you should look upon Him as your own loving Father; and that, however unworthy you may be, you should call yourself His beloved child. There cannot be a possible doubt of this, since it is taught so positively and uniformly by His only begotten Son, Who is "the Way, and the Truth, and the Life."†

If therefore, you desire to live in conformity with the New Law, which was made for you, you must no longer see God in the light in which the Jews saw Him: but you must see in Him a tender Father, and endeavour to cultivate filial feelings toward Him. In other words, you must now serve God in the spirit of love, and not of fear; for, as the Apostle St. Paul tells you, in the most positive manner: "You have not received the spirit of bondage again in fear; but you have received the spirit of adoption of sons, whereby we cry: Abba (Father)."‡

Even from a worldly point of view it is not good for us to be out of harmony with the times in which we live. Imagine, for instance, a man of our days so foolishly in love with the manners and customs of the thirteenth century as to insist that himself and family shall live after the

* Eph. iii. 15.   † St. John xiv. 6.   ‡ Rom. viii. 15.

fashion of that period. He gives his children the education of those times, dresses them in the singular costume then in vogue, and forces them to speak a language which no one can understand. In the event of war, he must buckle on strange armour, and with heavy sword and cumbersome shield, do battle against an enemy skilled in the use of the most improved fire-arms. Evidently, this man would be entirely out of harmony with the present age, to his own great inconvenience, and perhaps to that of others. And yet, it is very certain that this mode of warfare, this language and costume were all excellent in their day. But that day having passed away, no one can revive them without untold vexations and inconvenience to himself and those with whom he is in daily intercourse.

The same holds good in spiritual matters, especially among those who are aiming at Christian perfection—whether in the world or in the cloister. If, in spite of the expressed will of God to look upon Him as your Father, and to serve Him in a spirit of filial love, you insist upon viewing Him as the Jews did—almost exclusively as a terrible Judge, your manner of serving Him will never be perfect. You will, indeed, dread Him as the Jews did; you will tremble at the thought of Him; but you will never have a tender and filial love for Him. There will exist no familiarity between you and Him ; no sunshine will visit your soul : yea, and your very virtues will sicken even unto death. And why all this? Because you are entirely out of harmony with the New Law, which commands you to look upon God as your Father. You are battling exclusively with weapons that were good in their day, but are no longer so. You are evidently under a great disadvantage, and no words can tell the harm which must inevitably follow—injury to yourself, and annoyance to others, especially to your spiritual directors.

Moreover, your progress in the spiritual life is slow, perhaps almost imperceptible, because under the influence of your gloomy views of God, you drag yourself along slowly and painfully, instead of running and even flying, as you would do, were you thoroughly imbued with "the spirit of adoption of sons"—which is a spirit of love. "For God hath not given us the spirit of fear : but of power, and love."[*]

Remember, then, that you are not under the Old Law ; that you are not of the Jewish people. You are a Christian, and consequently a member of that newly chosen people of God, whom St. Peter addresses in these beautiful words:

[*] 2 Tim. i. 7.

"You are a chosen generation, a kingly priesthood, a holy nation, a purchased people; that you may declare His virtues, Who hath called you out of darkness into His marvellous light. Who in time past were not a people: but are now the people of God. Who had not obtained mercy; but now have obtained mercy."* Yes, Christian soul, this is the people of which you have the honour and the happiness of being a member. Accustom yourself to walk in the true spirit of so favoured a generation. This you will do by acknowledging God as your Father. Under the influence of this cheering view of God your whole interior will experience a wonderful change, and you will, even in this life, enjoy a foretaste of heaven; for you will begin to "taste and see that the Lord is sweet."†

What then, you will ask, becomes of that fear of God so often recommended in the Holy Scriptures? Is not the fear of the Lord still the very beginning of wisdom? Are not even the saints called upon to fear God? "Fear the Lord, all ye His Saints!"‡ Even so are they still exhorted to do; even so must they fear the Lord so long as they remain in this world of trial. For, though viewing God as our Father is in perfect harmony with the Gospel, it by no means follows that we must banish

* 1 St. Peter ii. 9.   † Ps. xxxiii. 9   ‡ *Ibid.* 10.

all fear of God from our hearts. They who should so understand the Gospel would be perverting the most consoling teachings of Jesus Christ into a cause of reprobation. They should certainly be classed among those "unlearned and unstable" men mentioned by St. Peter, "Who wrest the Scriptures to their own destruction."

There is no denying that the teachings of our Blessed Lord on this very subject have been misunderstood, and perverted by giving to the goodness, mercy, and compassion of God such exclusive prominence as to ignore, if not to deny altogether, His Divine justice in punishing sin. Such ideas of God's goodness are as dangerous as the austere views against which this whole book is directed. Nay, they are even more dangerous; for by thus considering God almost exclusively in His infinite goodness, and shutting our eyes against the exactions of His justice, we gradually begin to attribute to Him the weakness so often seen in over-indulgent parents, who excuse all the faults of their children, and can never find it in their hearts to punish them.

Such false views do even more. They insensibly lead to a contempt of God, and finally to a total denial of any eternal punishment hereafter. This is precisely the misfortune which has befallen Protestants. When they first departed from the unity of the Church they indulged in the most exaggerated descriptions of God's severity in punishing sin. So alarming and appalling were their frantic declamations that many, after losing all hopes of salvation, became confirmed maniacs. But a reaction is taking place in our day, and they are fast losing the little faith which they had retained from the Catholic Church. They now teach openly, both from the pulpit and through the press, that there is no hell, no eternal punishment for sin hereafter. God, say they, is too good to punish a creature for ever. They teach that the adulterer, the midnight assassin, the robber, and the like, who die without repentance, and in open rebellion against their God, will eventually be the bosom companions of the apostles, martyrs, holy virgins, and others who have led virtuous lives and deserved the "crown of justice" thereby. All the passages of Holy Scripture, which are so plain and emphatic on that subject, they have distorted into some other meaning, or explained entirely away. Hence, many of them have unfortunately succeeded in banishing all fear of God from their hearts, and some, alas ! all virtue, except such exterior appearances as may make them seem respectable in the eyes of the world.

We must, therefore, never lull to sleep that

salutary fear of God which keeps watch over our hearts. This might be the greatest misfortune that could befall us in this world. To love God tenderly, supremely, and without a particle of fear, is a blessedness reserved for us in our heavenly home. But so long as we remain pilgrims here below, we must never try, nor even desire, to lose that fear which is the beginning of wisdom.

The greatest saints, however pure and mortified, how gifted soever they were with the highest contemplation, never rose so high as to lose all fear of God. Even the Blessed Virgin Mary, immaculate though she was, was penetrated with the fear of the Lord; for she was filled with all the gifts of the Holy Ghost, and as the fear of the Lord is one of them, she undoubtedly possessed that one as well as the rest. Nay, more. Even Jesus Christ, in His human nature, was penetrated with a holy fear of God, His eternal Father. The prophet Isaiah, foretelling the wonderful gifts which should adorn the soul of the Redeemer, distinctly mentions the fear of the Lord as one of them. "And the Spirit of the Lord shall rest upon Him: the spirit of wisdom, and of understanding, the spirit of counsel, and of fortitude, the spirit of knowledge, and of godliness. And He shall be filled with the spirit of the fear of the Lord."*

You need not, therefore, imagine that viewing God as your Father will ever banish all fear of Him from your heart. The fear of God being a gift of the Holy Ghost suited to our present state of existence, cannot be dispensed with, and we should pray for this salutary fear every day of our lives.

But, then, this must be a filial fear, which is the legitimate offspring of an ardent love for God. Such a fear does not fill the mind with gloom or dread; neither does it dry up the springs of devotion. It does not disturb our peace, and much less does it ever impede our progress in the path of perfection. It is, on the contrary, a help, according to the words of the Holy Ghost: "The fear of the Lord shall delight the heart, and shall give joy, and gladness, and length of days. With him that feareth the Lord, it shall go well in the latter end, and in the day of his death he shall be blessed."*

Such a fear of God is not only desirable, but is even indispensable so long as we live in mortal flesh; and it is precisely such a wholesome fear as this which flows spontaneously from the habit of viewing God as our Father. It is the ever faithful companion of filial love, and is to be found in all good children, who greatly fear to offend their father—not so much because he has power to chastise, and even to disinherit them, but because they love him. St. Teresa speaks much of the great fear which she had of God. And though she received from Him the greatest of favours, and was often caressed by Him as a beloved child, she, nevertheless, retained a holy fear of Him even to her last breath.

Such, then, is the idea of God which we must endeavour to form in our mind if we desire to be in harmony with the Gospel. And as we are taught to cherish it, both by Jesus Christ Himself and by His Apostles, whom He commissioned to teach His doctrine, it must, of necessity, be the true one. God is our Father, and we must cultivate filial feelings toward Him; but He still remains our Sovereign Lord and Judge, and we must fear Him. Nevertheless, if we endeavour to see Him habitually in the light of a Father, as He desires, our fear will be tempered into a sweet, joyful, filial fear, which may, indeed, prevent us from falling into sin, but will never interfere with our love, unless, perhaps, it be to increase it more and more.

CHAPTER V.

GOD IS OUR FATHER BECAUSE HE IS OUR CREATOR.

HAVING seen that to view God as our Father is in perfect harmony with the teachings of the Gospel, we must now endeavour to imbue our minds more thoroughly with this consoling truth. In order to do so we must meditate upon it, and revolve it over and over again in our thoughts, until it makes a deep and lasting impression, and becomes one of our living convictions. It is only thus that this truth can have a telling influence upon our heart and life.

When we contemplate God creating man, we find that among the many thoughts that crowd upon us there are two which remain uppermost in our minds. Both are true and salutary. Both should be fostered with care, and never allowed to depart from our bosom. They are like twin sisters who live together in perfect harmony, and bring every blessing by their united presence, but are sure to produce evil if separated from each other.

The first of these thoughts is that we are the servants of the Most High; for by the act of creation God becomes our Sovereign Lord. He is our Master, and we are His property. As the clay is in the hands of the potter, so are we in the hands of God. His dominion over us is supreme, and the thought of questioning His right to command us whatsoever He pleases never enters our minds. Standing in the presence of our Divine Master, and contemplating His majesty and power, we are filled with awe, reverence, and fear. A feeling of willing submission comes over us; for we see clearly that it is perfectly reasonable that a servant should be subject and obedient to His Lord.

The second thought, inseparable from this, is that while remaining our Sovereign Lord, God is also our Father, not only because He has called us into existence, but also because, by an act of unutterable love, He has created us to His own image and likeness. This constitutes Him our Father, in the natural order, in a sense deeper than ever entered our minds, or ever will in this world. This is the sweet thought which fills our hearts with a tender love for God our heavenly Father. It is from this point of view that we are now to meditate upon the great mystery of our creation, and, without ignoring or forgetting that God is our Lord, we shall see that He is also our Father, because He is our Creator.

We are accustomed to call father the man whom the providence of God has selected as an instrument to bring us into existence. And we are certainly right; for God Himself calls him so, and commands us to honour, obey, and love him as such. Yet, if we closely examine his claims to paternity we find them very limited when compared to those of God. In fact, they dwindle into insignificance in the presence of God's claims to be called our Father.

Our earthly father is certainly no more than the instrument of our existence; he is not the author of it. He did not, and could not, fashion our wonderful frame, with its bones, sinews, arteries, veins, or its various members. Still less could he bestow upon us our senses, or send the life-blood coursing through our veins. Still less could he breathe into that wonderful and complicated structure our soul, that immortal image of the Living God, endowed as it is with its memory, intelligence and free-will. None of these things did our father according to the flesh create or bestow. Such a thought never even entered his mind.

If we now turn to our mother and ask what part she had in our creation, she answers, with the noble mother of the Machabees: "I know not how you were formed in my womb: for I neither gave you breathe, nor life, neither did I frame the limbs of every one of you. But the Creator of the world."* Yes, God alone created you, and He alone gave you whatever you possess in your soul or body. Your earthly parents could not have planted even one hair upon your head, nor can they replace even one of the many that fall. All men, taken together, with all their learning, ingenuity and cunning, could not make the most insignificant insect, much less give it life. Man, however great and powerful in other respects, is totally powerless when there is question of creating.

God alone, then, by His power, wisdom, and love, called you into existence, and made you the noblest and most perfect of all visible creatures. He is, therefore, your Father in a sense far deeper than you can ever fathom, while your earthly father dwindles into an instrument used by Him to give you the existence which you now enjoy.

But this is not all. When once created, our earthly father did not, and could not, give us growth, strength, and health. He laboured and cared for us with love, it is true, but he did not create either the food or the raiment he gave us. It was our heavenly Father Who created and placed within his reach whatever he gave us for the sustenance and comfort of life. Yes, it was

* 2 Mach. vii. 22.

your heavenly Father, "Who maketh His sun to rise upon the good and bad, and raineth upon the just and the unjust," that gave growth to all the necessaries of life. Neither your father, nor all men taken together, could create a morsel of bread or a fibre of raiment. Here again, then, as well as in your creation, your earthly father appears in the capacity of an instrument in the hands of your heavenly Father, Who alone has preserved you, and Who alone can continue to do so. Certainly, then, the great, wise, and good God, to Whom you owe your whole being and its preservation, is truly your Father.

But, again, there comes a day, in this world, when we no longer need an earthly father. We become of age, fully developed in mind and body, and, therefore, fully competent to take care of ourselves. We are independent—so very independent that we can leave home and go where we please to build our fortunes—even across the seas, where a father's care will never reach us. Yea, we may even see the day when age and infirmity will make our father totally dependent on us. In his second childhood, we shall be obliged to care for him with all charity, and do for him what he did for us when we were helpless little children.

Oh! how different are the relations in which we stand toward our heavenly Father! Never will there come a time, either in this world or in the next, when we shall be of age, and shall no longer need His upholding hand. Never will there dawn a day of independence; never a day, nor even an hour, when we shall be so fully grown and developed as to be sufficient for ourselves. Never shall we be able to leave the home of His right hand, and take care of ourselves without Him. We need Him now as much as we did on the first day of our existence; and when as many ages will have rolled by as there are drops of water in the ocean, and grains of sand on the sea-shore, we shall still need Him as much as we now do, "for in Him we live and move and be."* And were He, at any time, to withdraw His hand from us, even for an instant, we should immediately fall back into our original nothingness, and be no more; no, not as much as the insignificant insect which we now trample under foot.

God, then, is our Father in a sense so true, and yet so deep, that we have no words to give it adequate expression. The filial tie and the total dependence which we contract on the very first day of our existence is never broken; no, never. And it shall not be broken, even if by repeated and continued rebellions against our heavenly Father, we compel him to disinherit us, and disown us for ever. For even then shall we still depend totally upon Him for our wretched existence. Such, then, is God our Father, creating, preserving, and upholding us with infinite power and wisdom, with a mysterious and unspeakable love.

But you may say: If God is our Father, because He is our Creator, is He not also the Father of every creature, of the sun, moon, and stars, and of the earth beneath them? God is the Author of all creation. In this sense we find in the Holy Scriptures, the words Father, Creator, and Maker often used as having the same meaning. For instance, God speaking to Job from the whirlwind, asks: "Who is the father of the rain? or who begot the drops of dew?"* Again, Moses, upbraiding the children of Israel for their ingratitude to God, says: "Is this the return thou makest to the Lord, O foolish and senseless people? Is not He thy Father, that hath possessed thee, and made thee, and created thee?"† And again, the prophet Isaiah, praying for his people, speaks thus: "And now, O Lord, Thou art our Father, and we are clay: and Thou art our Maker, and we are the works of Thy hands."‡ And so in other parts of Holy Scripture.

But when we say that God is our Father because He is our Creator, we do not mean to assert that, in the act of creation we are made partakers of the Divine nature, as we are of the human nature of our parents. Much less do we mean to assert that God is our Father in the same sense as He is Father to His only begotten Son. For, according to the beautiful words of the Nicene Creed, that Son is "born of the Father before all ages. God of God, Light of Light, true God of true God; begotten, not made; consubstantial with the Father, by Whom all things were made." In such a sublime and strictly literal sense as this, God neither is, nor can He be, our Father. Hence, when we say that God is our Father because He is our Creator, we must take it in the sense in which He Himself understands it when He calls Himself the "one God and Father of all, Who is above all, and through all, and in us all."*

Moreover, though it be true that, in a certain sense, God may be called the Father of all Creation, He is called so, principally, if not exclusively, in reference to man. First, because man alone can know this truth and love God as his Father. Secondly, in speaking of God's paternity in creatures, we must not merely take into account the bare act of creation, but also the amount of resemblance to Himself which God has stamped upon the works of His hands. As irrational and inanimate creatures are not, properly speaking, images of God, but rather mirrors reflecting some of His attributes in an inferior degree, there is, as St. Thomas says, only a vestige of God's paternity to be seen in them. They cannot, therefore, with propriety be called children of God, though He is their Creator as well as ours. Hence, when our Blessed Lord says: "Behold the birds of the air, for they neither sow, nor do they reap, nor gather into barns," He does not add their heavenly Father feedeth them, but "your heavenly Father feedeth them."

But the case is quite different when there is question of man; for God has stamped His likeness upon him in so striking a manner that he is, in very deed, the living image of the Most High. Hence, we alone of all visible creatures can say: "The light of Thy countenance, O Lord, is signed upon us."* Our soul, which, by its very nature, is immortal, and is endowed with intelligence, free-will, and other God-like attributes, gives us a right to be called children of God in a far stricter sense than other creatures.

But to return. What is the first instinct of a child toward its earthly parents? One of love, is it not? Certainly. And we should look upon him as a monster in nature, who does not love his parents; for it is a law written by the hand of God in the heart of every child that enters this world. And we love our parents, too, though we know full well how little they had to do with our existence and preservation. We love them, too, in spite of the many imperfections, shortcomings, and even grievous sins we may discover in them. We love them because they are the instruments of our existence, because they first loved us, and did what they could for us. They have thus acquired an undeniable claim to our love, which we freely give.

Now, if all this be so, as undeniably it is, what shall we say of our heavenly Father's claim to our love? Has He not done infinitely more than our earthly parents ever did for us? Has He not loved us infinitely more than they ever did, or even than they ever can? Their finite love, however ardent it may be, disappears almost entirely when compared with the infinite love of our heavenly Father, which reaches from eternity to eternity.

Yes, Christian reader, your heavenly Father loved you from all eternity, before you had an existence, except in His mind: "Yea, I have loved thee with everlasting love, therefore have I drawn thee, taking pity on thee."* Nay, the very fact of your existing now, is an unbroken act of love on the part of God. Listen to the beautiful words of the Wise Man: "For Thou lovest all things that are, and hatest none of the things which Thou hast made. For Thou didst

* Jerem. xxxi. 3.

not appoint, or make anything, hating it. And how could anything endure, if Thou wouldst not? or be preserved, if not called by Thee? But Thou sparest all: because they are Thine, O Lord, Who lovest souls."

But this is not all. We have seen that we love our earthly father, even when we discover in him deformity, imperfection, and sin. But our love is certainly intensified, if that man, besides being our father, is possessed of great personal beauty, learning, wisdom, holiness, and every other perfection that makes one truly great and noble. If so, what shall we say of the love we should have for our heavenly Father? For in Him are united, in an infinite degree, all imaginable perfections. And now let me close this chapter by laying before you a beautiful picture of God, drawn by the master-hand of a recent but well known convert to the Church.

Speaking of the teachings of theology, he says: "I mean, then, by the Supreme Being, One Who is simply self-dependent, and the only Being Who is such; moreover, that He is without beginning, or Eternal, and the only Eternal: that in consequence He has lived a whole eternity by Himself; and hence, that He is all-sufficient, sufficient for His own blessedness, and all-blessed, and ever-blessed. Further, I mean a Being, Who, having these prerogatives, has the

Supreme Good, or rather, is the Supreme Good, or has all the attributes of Good in infinite intenseness; all wisdom, all truth, all justice, all love, all holiness, all beautifulness; Who is omnipotent, omniscient, omnipresent, ineffably one, absolutely perfect; and such, that what we do not know and cannot even imagine of Him, is far more wonderful than what we do and can. I mean One Who is Sovereign over His own will and actions, though always according to the eternal Rule of right and wrong, which is Himself. I mean, moreover, that He created all things out of nothing, and preserves them at every moment, and could destroy them as easily as He made them; and that, in consequence, He is separated from them by an abyss, and is incommunicable in all His attributes. And further, He has stamped upon all things, in the hour of their creation, their respective natures, and has given them their work, and mission, and their length of days, greater or less, in their appointed place. I mean, too, that He is ever present with His works, one by one, and confronts everything He has made by His particular and most loving Providence, and manifests Himself to each according to its needs; and has, on rational beings, imprinted the moral law, and given them power to obey it, imposing upon them the duty of worship and service, searching and scanning them through and through with His omniscient eye, and putting before them a present trial, and a judgment to come.

"Such is what theology teaches about God. . . . It teaches of a Being infinite, yet personal; all-blessed, yet ever operative; absolutely separate from the creature, yet in every part of the creation at every moment; above all things, yet under everything. It teaches of a Being Who, though the highest, yet in the work of creation, conservation, government, retribution, makes Himself, as it were, the minister and servant of all; Who, though inhabiting eternity, allows Himself to take an interest and to feel a sympathy in the matters of space and time." *

This is certainly a grand and sublime picture of God. Look upon it often, and you will find yourself loving Him spontaneously. You will even feel a noble pride at the thought that your heavenly Father is so great, so beautiful, wise, good, holy, so completely and unspeakably perfect. For this is neither a one-sided nor a narrow-minded view of God. Every divine attribute is here presented as infinite; not one is either ignored, or exaggerated so as to eclipse the others. He is our God, our Sovereign Lord, King and Judge, but He is also our most compassionate Father, because He is our Creator.

* Dr. Newman's Second University Discourse.

CHAPTER VI.

GOD IS OUR FATHER BECAUSE HE HAS ADOPTED US IN JESUS CHRIST.

HAVING seen that God is our Father because He is our Creator, we shall now endeavour to see how He becomes our Father in the order of grace. By an act of unspeakable mercy and goodness, He has adopted us in Jesus Christ, His own Son, and bestowed upon us the rights and privileges of children in the supernatural order—the order of grace and glory. It is of this glorious adoption, and of its effects, that we shall now speak.

What is the meaning of adoption? It means the taking, as our own, the children of others, and putting them on a footing of equality with our own. But these are cold words, and almost meaningless when used in reference to our adoption as children of God in the supernatural order. Let us have recourse to a little illustration which will throw more light upon the subject than abstract words could do.

Let us suppose a great and mighty king, who, of his own goodness, elevates to respectability a man and woman, whose lot was cast by nature in the lowest walks of life. He places them in a magnificent palace; gives them immense tracts of land, silver, gold, and jewels, and whatever else may contribute to their happiness. All these gifts they may enjoy, and, moreover, transmit to their children, and to their children's children, on condition, however, that they acknowledge their dependence on the good king by obeying him in one command both easy and just. They, of course, promise obedience; but, after some time of enjoyment, both of them, by a positive act of disobedience, refuse to fulfil the necessary conditions to their happiness. Now, it is evident that, by this one act of disobedience, they themselves, as well as their children, have forfeited all right and title to the wealth, position, and happiness which continued fidelity to the king would have secured to them.

Let us now suppose, further, that after some time the king adopts one of their children. He is poor, neglected, and ignorant. But the king clothes him as his own, educates him, and prepares wealth, position, and happiness of the highest order—all of which he is to enjoy when he is of age. Now, I ask, could that fortunate boy call the king his father? Undoubtedly he could; and he certainly would view him in that light, and love him, too, with a love even more tender than he could have for his father according to the flesh.

This illustration speaks better than words, and all you have to do is to substitute God for the king, Adam and Eve for the man and woman, and yourself for the adopted child. Then will you begin to see and to understand how God becomes your Father in the order of grace, and how you really became His child, with all the rights and privileges of children. But did God, in fact, so adopt us? Did He, by this adoption, restore to us what we had lost by the prevarication of Adam? Yes, He did restore all, and even more; so much so, that the Church, in an ecstasy of wonder and delight, sings, "O felix culpa!"—O happy fall, which deserved for us so great a Redeemer!

We shall now examine a few of the most striking passages of Holy Scripture, which tell us of our adoption as children of God in the order of grace, and of the supernatural happiness which follows it. Here is one to which your special attention is called: "But when the fulness of time was come, God sent His Son, made of a woman, made under the law, that He might redeem them who were under the law; that we might receive the adoption of sons. And because you are sons, God hath sent the Spirit of His Son into your hearts, crying: Abba, Father,"* This is certainly plain and emphatic language. It would be difficult to find a truth more clearly or more powerfully expressed. The passage needs neither comment nor explanation, for there is no doubt as to its real meaning. It asserts simply that, by adoption, we are the children of God; that in virtue of this adoption, we have a right to view God as our own Father; and that we have, in consequence, the obligation of loving Him as our Father, and of cultivating filial feelings toward Him.

And this looking upon ourselves as God's children, must not be understood as a mere figure of speech, which does not really mean what it says. For it does most certainly mean what it asserts in its natural and literal sense; and it is confirmed in that sense by other passages of Scripture which can easily be adduced. Here is another, taken from St. John, the Apostle whom Jesus loved. We shall see whether he understands it in a figurative or a literal sense: "Behold what manner of charity the Father hath bestowed upon us, that we should be called, and should be the sons of God. . . . Dearly beloved, we are now the sons of God; and it hath not yet appeared what we shall be. We know that when He

* Galat. iv.

shall appear, we shall be like Him, because we shall see Him as He is."*

This passage is, if possible, still more precise and positive than the preceding. Moreover, it gives us a glimpse of the unspeakable glory that is to follow as the legitimate consequence of our adoption. For, by becoming children of God, we are again clothed with a right to possess and enjoy the heavenly inheritance which we had lost in the fall of our first parents. Our adoption restores to us the right to enter heaven, not as beggars, but as children who go into their father's house as into their own. Of this St. Paul assures us in his usual forcible manner: "For the Spirit Himself giveth testimony to our spirit, that we are the sons of God. And if sons, heirs also: heirs, indeed, of God, and joint-heirs with Christ."† How consoling must be so glorious a privilege, when we reflect upon it! We, poor disinherited sons of Adam, are elevated and made co-heirs with Jesus Christ! We should envy the happy lot of a poor boy who is adopted by a king of this world, because high privileges, happiness and glory follow such an adoption. Nevertheless, all these favours, taken together, "are not worthy to be compared with the glory to come, that shall be revealed in us."‡ For the inheritance to which his adop-

* 1 St. John iii.   † Rom. viii. 16.   ‡ Rom. viii. 18.

tion gives him a right, how great and desirable soever it may be, is, after all, a corruptible one, which a few short years will cause to fade away and perish; while ours is "an inheritance incorruptible and undefiled, and that cannot fade."*

But this is not all. When there is question of the order of grace, God is our Father in a sense more sublime. He is not our Father merely because He bestows upon us a right to an eternal inheritance; He is our Father also, because, "Of His own will, He hath begotten us by the word of truth,"† and because, also, we are born of Him. It is St. John who teaches us this sublime truth. Speaking of those who received the Saviour, he says: "As many as received Him, He gave them the power to be made the sons of God, to them that believe in His name. Who are born, not of blood, nor of the will of the flesh, nor of the will of man, but of God."‡ Perhaps we could never have dared to imagine, and much less to believe so consoling a truth, were it not so clearly stated in the Holy Scriptures.

Besides, in speaking of God as our Father in the order of nature, we carefully noticed that, in the act of our creation, we did not become "partakers of the Divine nature," but only of the nature of our earthly parents. But the

* 1 St. Peter i. 5.   † St. James i. 18.   ‡ St. John i. 12.

case is quite different when we speak of Him as our Father in the order of grace. For in the act whereby, "of His own will He hath begotten us," He has also communicated Himself to us in so wonderful a manner as to make us "partakers of the Divine Nature."* This is the unlooked for honour and high privilege which seems to crown all the other supernatural gifts of our heavenly Father. It imprints upon us a character of resemblance to God far greater and more perfect than that in which we were created, and it is second only to that likeness which shall be revealed in us when "we shall be like Him, because we shall see Him as He is." For it is the communication of Himself in the Beatific Vision which will complete and perfect the resemblance begun here by the gifts of grace, and cause us to shine like God unto all eternity. "In other things," says Father Lessius, "as in the fabric of the world, and various degrees of things, certain thin rays of His Divinity shine forth, from which we can, as it were by conjecture, learn His power, His wisdom, and His goodness. But in our minds, elevated by the light of glory, and united to Him in the Beatific Vision, the whole plenitude of the Divinity shines forth, the whole of His beauty softly glows; so that, although the Divinity is one in itself, it is in a marvellous

* 2 St. Peter i. 4.

manner multiplied, so that there seem to be as many Divinities as there are beatified minds."

But, again. Not only do we become, indeed, and in very truth, children of the Living God by this adoption, but, by a natural consequence, we also become the brethren of Jesus Christ. It is our Blessed Lord Himself Who teaches us this consoling truth by styling us His own brethren. "Amen, I say to you, as long as you did it to one of these, My least brethren, you did it to Me."* And, again, rising gloriously from the dead, He appears to Mary Magdalen, and says to her: "Go to My brethren, and say to them, I ascend to My Father, and to your Father, to My God, and to your God."†

It is evident, then, Christian reader, that God is really your Father in the order of grace. For, as in the order of nature, neither father nor mother could, of themselves, have given you existence, so, in the order of grace, neither priest nor bishop, nor even the Pope, could have given you the spiritual life you now enjoy. They were, indeed, instruments in the hands of your heavenly Father, and they, no doubt, performed, with fidelity, the solemn rite of baptism. But it was He alone Who gave you life. You were conceived and born in sin, but now according to the emphatic words of the Apostle, "You are

* St. Matt. xxv. 40.   † St. John xx. 17.

washed. . . . You are sanctified. . . . You are justified in the name of our Lord Jesus Christ, and the Spirit of our God."* It was He alone Who clothed you in the robe of innocence, and made you beautiful as the very angels who stand around His throne. It was He alone Who infused into you sanctifying grace, faith, hope, and charity, and made you His own child.

Even if you are a convert, and were already full grown when baptized, it was all His work. No doubt, you prepared yourself by prayer, and by a true sorrow for your sins; but it was He Who, by enlightening your mind, enabled you to believe. The gift of faith, the life, the adoption, the new birth—all came from God alone, as well as your creation.

But we have not yet done with God's paternity in the order of grace. Who preserved you in that life of grace which your heavenly Father bestowed upon you on the day of your baptism? Certainly it was not yourself. For, as when once created, you could not suffice for yourself, but needed food and raiment, which all came from God, so, also, in the supernatural life which you have received, you depend totally on God for its preservation. So completely dependent on Him are you in the order of grace, that you cannot, of yourself, even think a good

* 1 Cor. vi. 11.

thought. This is what St. Paul teaches : "Not that we are sufficient to think anything of ourselves, as of ourselves ; but our sufficiency is from God."*

Here again, then, God is your Father, because He is continually preserving that precious life of grace, which He bestowed upon you on the day of your baptism. And when, by wilful mortal sin, you lose that life, it is your heavenly Father Who still preserves in you the light of faith, and the virtue of hope, and lovingly prepares the grace that may bring back to His bosom the prodigal child. For you are, by yourself alone, as powerless to restore to yourself the life of grace, as the corpse is to restore itself to life. You, therefore, depend totally on God, not only for your adoption, and the glorious privileges it involves, but also for your preservation in that adoption. God is, therefore, your Father, in a sense so true, so elevated and sublime, that we have no language to give it adequate expression.

When we reflect seriously upon all this, and endeavour to conceive it fully, we are filled with awe at seeing ourselves so near to God, and His children in so real and so deep a sense. But we are also filled with a most tender love for so great a God, Who, out of His own deep love for us, has condescended to elevate us to the rank

* 2 Cor. iii. 5.

of children. We no longer feel inclined to look upon God habitually as an inexorable Judge, ever holding the rod of justice, but as a most loving Father, Who, while He commands us to fear Him with a filial fear, also commands us to love Him, and even condescends to reveal a mysterious craving for the trifling measure of love which we can give to His Divine Majesty.

CHAPTER VII.

VIEWING GOD AS OUR FATHER IS OF THE GREATEST HELP TO US IN THE TIME OF SPIRITUAL DESOLATION.

HAVING shown that God is our Father, because He is our Creator, and also because He has adopted us in Jesus Christ, thereby elevating us to the supernatural order, we shall now examine some of the happy results which flow to the souls of those who bear in mind this consoling truth, and who make it a point to consider God habitually in the light of a tender Father. One of these results is patience, resignation, and interior peace in the various trials which attend the spiritual life; and, especially, in the subtraction of all sensible devotion. But, before entering upon the subject, I wish it to be distinctly understood that, in all I am about to say, there is no reference whatever to the awful mystical trials of which we read so much in the lives of the saints. My intention is to speak of such trials only as are common to all, or nearly all, Christians who are aiming at Christian perfection, whether in the world or in religious communities.

It is said by a great servant of God, that the entering upon a pious life is very much like the entering into a well-cultivated garden, filled with beautiful flowers, choice fruit-bearing trees, singing birds, cool springs, and whatever else can recreate the senses, and fill the soul with innocent pleasure. But, after some time of enjoyment, we perceive that the flowers begin to lose their freshness, beauty, and perfume. The fruits, also, which at first were so delicious, now become tasteless, and even sour. The birds no longer sing so sweetly, and, after awhile, they have no song. The cooling springs are gradually dried up, and, finally, we find ourselves in a vast barren wilderness, almost destitute of everything that can make life comfortable.

The great majority of Christians aiming at Christian perfection, are to pass through this wilderness, and to remain in it a longer or shorter time according to God's particular dispensation to each one of His children. Some there are who die while yet in their first fervour, and go to their heavenly home like little children who die before they know anything of the troubles and cares of life. But the majority of pious people live long enough to enter the wilderness. It is therefore, of this spiritual wilderness we are now to speak, and we shall see that to look upon God as our Father is a great help to us in bearing patiently, and even joyfully, the trials and hardships which in this wilderness are of daily occurrence.

While our first fervour lasted, we had a supernatural promptitude and ease in all that belongs to the service of God. We could "pray always," and that with few or no distractions. We had a facility in meditation, and in keeping our thoughts upon spiritual things; in fact, good thoughts, heavenly thoughts, came to us spontaneously, and remained with us without effort on our part. We then felt great sweetness in prayer, and joy in the sacraments. We could easily perform penances, and submit to humiliations. We were troubled with but few temptations, and these we could manage with perfect ease. In a word, we lived with God, and at times we fancied we could almost see and touch Him, so near to us did He seem, so intimate were we with Him. We saw in Him so much beauty and goodness, that we loved Him generously and ardently. We even wondered how it was possible for any one not to love Him as we did, and we were, in consequence, not unfrequently harsh in our judgments of others.

But this first fervour, with all its sweetness and poetry, has passed away, probably never to return; and it has left us in the great, cold wilderness. How changed seems everything around us! And how changed we ourselves seem! We can scarcely recognize our former selves. Even God seems to have changed. We no longer see Him in so beautiful and captivating a light, and we do not, and cannot, love Him as we once did. He seems to have gone away from us; for we no longer feel His Divine presence in our soul. Our prayers, too, have become dry, distracted and wearisome. We feel no sensible devotion in the sacraments, and we even fancy, at times, that we have almost lost our very faith. Our passions, which we thought dead and buried, now seem stronger and more unmanageable than ever. The world, too, which we had so heartily despised, now puts on charms so captivating and seems so capable of giving us perfect happiness, that we feel strongly tempted to give up all our practices of devotion, and plunge headlong into its pleasures. In a word, we have lost all sensible devotion and relish for spiritual things, and we must now drag ourselves by main force to do what is of strict obligation. If to all this we add wrong views of God, and persist in looking upon Him principally as an inexorable Judge, our state will be distressing indeed, and deserving of compassion.

This, then, is the state of spiritual existence through which most pious people pass, after their first fervour is taken from them. Some suffer more, and some less; but it is for all without exception, a state of trial and interior suffering. The suffering, however, or the gloom at least, is much lessened, if we view this state in the right light, and have our views of God in harmony with the Gospel.

First of all, this is not such a bad state as most people imagine it to be. It is no evidence that we have lost God's favour, or that we are less holy in his sight than we were when we abounded to overflowing with spiritual consolations. The very reverse is most probably the truth; for as this spiritual desolation is a particular dispensation of God's providence to all who give themselves to His service in good earnest, it must also be a means of sanctifying grace, which does its work as well as the far more pleasant state of sensible fervour. Hence, how gloomy soever all things may appear to you, and how unpleasant soever all this may be to your natural inclination, it is nevertheless brought about by your heavenly Father for your greater good and higher sanctification. I must, therefore, tell you in the words of the Apostle: "And we helping do exhort you, that you receive not the grace of God in vain. . . . Behold now is the acceptable time: behold now is the day of salvation."*

* 2 Cor. vi. 1.

If, in the second place, you accustom yourself to look upon God as your Father, this subtraction of all sensible devotion, these annoying distractions, these troublesome temptations, as well as your involuntary distaste for spiritual things, will appear to you in a light which will make them, to say the best, very tolerable. For then you will be sweetly resigned to the will of God, Who so ordains it. You will say with your Lord Jesus: "My Father, if it be possible, let this chalice pass from Me. Nevertheless, not as I will, but as Thou wilt."* This will be your prayer, and your dispositions will be in accordance with it. For seeing God as your Father, you will become intimately convinced that He has brought about this state of trial for your greater sanctification, to beautify your soul, to make you resemble Jesus Christ the more, and to fit you for a higher place in heaven.

What is the conduct of parents toward their children? They tear them away from their bosom, and from all the sweet pleasures of home, to send them far away in order to receive an education. The moment of separation is heartrending, but go they must, and that, too, among strangers, who, even if they would, can never have the hearts and feelings of parents toward

* St. Matt. xxvi. 39.

them. They must now, in their new position, observe so many rules, learn so many difficult lessons, submit to punishments sometimes apparently too great, and sometimes even altogether undeserved, and go through all the other annoyances, self-denials and hardships which are involved in the receiving of an education. But what is the ultimate result of all this? It is that the child, who had left home ignorant, returns a man. He is now educated, accomplished, and can present himself, with credit, in society. He is, moreover, competent to fill honourable positions, which he never could have done, had his father been so weak-minded as to listen to his lamentations, and allow him to remain without an education. Hence, howsoever sad and painful for the child was the separation, the long absence from home, and the hardships endured, the sending him away was, nevertheless, an act of love on the part of his father, for which he, on his return, is thankful.

It is thus that God acts toward His children in the order of grace. God being your Father by every imaginable title, loves you more tenderly than does your father according to the flesh. He is always, therefore, watching over you, and seeking your greater good. He tears you from His paternal embrace and sends you away from the sweet home of His bosom, that you may be schooled by His grace and developed into the image of Jesus Christ, "For whom He foreknew He also predestined to be made conformable to the image of His Son,"* Who, in His human nature, is the standard of created beauty, holiness and perfection; and it is only by becoming like Him, in a greater or less degree of perfection, that we can hope to be saved at all. But as our object, in leading a pious life, is not merely to be saved, but to attain, moreover, to a high degree of glory in heaven, it follows that our study must be to resemble our Lord Jesus Christ in a degree of perfection corresponding to the measure of grace imparted to us. It follows, also, that we must cheerfully submit to all the means which God makes use of to render us more and more perfect in the likeness of His Son.

Now, one of the means employed by our heavenly Father to bring about this desired end is this very subtraction of all sensible devotion. For it is by such trials as dryness in prayer, interior desolation, the most horrid and distressing temptations, and other kindred sufferings of the soul, that He gradually develops in us a most wonderful resemblance to Jesus

* Rom. viii. 29.

Christ. He thus educates, beautifies and perfects our souls, and fits them for the high position we are to occupy in the heavenly society. Such trials, therefore, instead of making us sad and despondent, ought to fill us with joy; for they are a most positive evidence of God's fatherly love for us. It is precisely because He loves you more than you can conceive that He presses to your lips the chalice of which His Son, Jesus Christ, and all His chosen ones had to drink. For it is a most remarkable fact that He has afflicted those who loved and served Him best, and that He has done so precisely because they were so dear to Him. Listen to the angel speaking to the holy patriarch, Tobias: "When thou didst pray with tears, and didst bury the dead, and didst leave thy dinner, and hide the dead by day in thy house, and bury them by night, I offered thy prayer to the Lord. And because thou wast acceptable to God, it was necessary that temptation should prove thee."* Here is certainly a just man, most dear to the heart of God, and, one would think, a man who should on that account be free from suffering, and yet he must be proved by temptation and sorrow. And what was the temptation?. It was that Tobias should, for a time, be deprived of his

* Tob. xii.

sight, one of the greatest afflictions of this life. And this trial comes upon him precisely because he is acceptable to God.

Listen also to the words which our blessed Lord spoke a few moments before His passion: "Amen, Amen, I say to you, that you shall lament and weep, but the world shall rejoice: and you shall be made sorrowful, but your sorrow shall be turned into joy."* It was not to His enemies He spoke thus. It was to His eleven chosen ones, whom He called friends, and to all who in course of time should endeavour to lead a holy life. He traced the path Himself in His own blood, and after Him followed His spotless Mother, drinking deeper of His chalice than any other mortal. Then came the apostles, the martyrs, the confessors, the holy virgins, and all others who lead pious lives, and aim at a distinguished place in the kingdom of His Father. It is plain, then, that the sufferings of this life are evidences of God's love for His children; and as spiritual desolation and absence of sensible devotion are a great suffering to a loving soul, it follows that they too are to be ranked among the marks of God's love for us. For they develop in the soul a more perfect resemblance to Jesus Christ than the sensible devotion of beginners could ever do.

* St. John xvi. 20.

But these trials do more in our soul. They deaden in us, or weaken, at least, those passions which would infallibly efface or deform the image of Christ in proportion as it is formed. Our bosom swarms with dangerous passions, and among them there is one which generally predominates over all others. It is called the predominant or ruling passion, because our most frequent and grievous faults can usually be traced to it, as to their source. In one, it is pride; in another, it is inordinate and dangerous attachments; in another, it is an ungoverned temper, and great uncharitableness to others, both in word and deed; while in others it is most dangerous self-trust. These last seem to forget that without God they are "wretched, and miserable, and poor, and blind, and naked."* Like Peter, they are full of confidence in their own strength and virtue, and in the sincerity of their resolution not to commit sin. They even come to look with contempt upon others whose exterior is, perhaps, not so polished as theirs, and the spirit of the Pharisee, who thanked God that he was not like other men, is gradually formed in them. And the worst is, that these good people only half see the dangerous character of these treacherous passions. Even in the supposition that they

* Apoc. iii. 17.

do see them, they are, for the most part, so cowardly that they have not the courage to attack them, and to fight manfully and master them.

This being so, what should you expect of God, if He is your Father? Is it that He should continue to inundate your soul with sensible devotion, and make you thereby still more self-conceited? Is it that He should shut His eyes and let these dangerous passions rule you, and drag you into perdition? Certainly not. You would rather expect Him either to kill them, or to give them well-aimed blows which should, at least render, them comparatively harmless. This is precisely what He does by sending you sufferings, humiliations, and other trials which you never would have had the courage to choose for yourself. This is what He does by taking away from you all sensible devotion, thus letting you see how utterly wretched you are when left to yourself. Evidently, then, such trials are a manifestation of God's tenderest love for you.

A certain young lady, whose father was a physician, had been for a long time suffering from a dreadful cancer. Having tried every remedy without success, the father became convinced that nothing but a very painful operation could save the life of his child. He sent the mother to prepare the child, and to induce her to submit to the operation willingly. The daughter listened for awhile, but soon interrupted the mother and said: "Mother, you need not use so many arguments. Since the operation is pronounced necessary by my father I submit to it willingly. He is my father, and I know he loves me very tenderly, and will perform this operation for my good. I know, moreover, that his heart will guide his hand in doing what must be done." What a beautiful disposition! And how very reasonable! She knew that this operation, however painful, was an act of love on the part of her father, and she, therefore, submitted without a murmur.

This is precisely the disposition of mind and heart that will gradually be formed in you, if you accustom yourself to look upon God as your Father. You will henceforth need very few, if any, arguments to make you submit willingly, and even cheerfully, to the privation of sensible devotion, and all other trials which belong to the spiritual life. When you are in darkness and worried with distractions in prayer; when legions of horrible thoughts rush into your mind unbidden, and in spite of yourself; when, even after Communion, such distressing and humiliating thoughts crowd upon you, and compel you to spend these precious moments in almost fruitless endeavours to banish them; when, finally, instead of devotion and spiritual sweetness, you feel a general distaste for all the pious practices which formerly were the source of so much consolation to you, you will, in spite of all this, remain in peace. You will say: "Since these trials are permitted, or sent by my heavenly Father, they certainly must be necessary for my good. They are, no doubt, intended to take away my pride, my confidence in myself, and to teach me that of myself I can do nothing. They reveal the fact that, without the assistance of divine grace, I cannot have even a good thought: I therefore submit to them all patiently, if not cheerfully. They are, indeed, a very painful operation, but I know that in all these trials, the heart of my heavenly Father guides His hand, and I look upon them as evidences of His love for me." These are the sentiments to be found in all persons who have accustomed themselves to look upon God as a tender Father.

But you say: "How happy I should be could I believe that my trials are evidences of God's love for me! How cheerfully would I then submit to be without sensible devotion, and to remain in darkness, temptation and suffering! But I have every reason to fear that they are only evidences of God's anger, and punishments which He inflicts upon me for my many sins and infidelities to grace." Well, suppose they are punishments, what then! Are they, therefore, marks of God's hatred toward you? Do they mean that you are excommunicated from the Heart of God? They certainly have no such meaning. When you see a father chastising his children, do you immediately infer that he no longer loves them, or that he even hates them? Such a thought never enters your mind. You know full well that he loves them, even while chastising them. You know that he inflicts the punishment precisely because he does love them; for his object is to correct them of defects which might eventually prove their ruin. So it is with your heavenly Father, when He chastises you. He loves you still, and inflicts the punishment precisely because He loves you. This is what St. Paul tells you in the most positive language: "For whom the Lord loveth He chastiseth: and He scourgeth every son whom He receiveth. Persevere under discipline. God dealeth with you as with His sons. For what son is there whom the father does not correct? But if you be without chastisement, whereof all are made partakers; then you are bastards and not sons."* This language is certainly plain and

---
* 1 Heb. xii.

emphatic enough to make you see that, even if your trials are merited punishments for your sins and infidelities, they are, nevertheless, evidences of your heavenly Father's love for you. While inflicting them, His heart guides His hand; for He loves you because you are His child. His object is to correct you of your defects, and to destroy in you dangerous passions which might prove your ruin, or which would certainly prevent the likeness of Christ being formed in you, except in a very inferior degree.

To view God, then, as our Father is evidently of great help to us in bearing all the trials and hardships, which are inseparable from the spiritual life. With that idea of God deeply impressed upon our minds, we shall bear them not only patiently, but also in a meritorious manner. For, besides forming the image of Christ in us, and correcting us of our defects, they increase our merits, "For that which is at present momentary and light of our tribulation, worketh for us above measure exceedingly an eternal weight of glory."* They will no longer impede our growth in holiness, nor fill us with gloom, nor make us despondent, nor take away our interior peace. They will, on the contrary, cause us to grow in sanctity more rapidly and solidly than we could under the influence of sensible devotion. In a word, the thought of God as our Father is the sunshine, that not only throws a golden light upon all the sufferings of this life, but, moreover, imparts to us in our spiritual growth that courage and vigour which are so necessary to fight the good fight, and to deserve the "Crown of Justice" promised to all who distinguish themselves in the practice of virtue.

CHAPTER VIII.

VIEWING GOD AS OUR FATHER PRODUCES PEACE OF CONSCIENCE AS TO OUR PAST SINS.

OF the many good results which flow to our souls from looking upon God as our Father, one of the best and most desirable is a child-like confidence that He has forgiven and forgotten our sins, and that they shall neither rise against us at the hour of death, nor follow us to judgment, there to call for our condemnation. This perfect confidence in the mercy of our heavenly Father fills the soul with "the peace of God, which surpasseth all understanding," and is one of the most precious gifts that can be enjoyed on earth. It is in reality, a foretaste of that deep, undisturbed peace which the Blessed enjoy in heaven. For, in that blessed country, the happy inhabitants neither have, nor can have, any doubt as to the forgiveness of their sins. They therefore enjoy, in its fullest extent, the peace which comes from God, and which can never be marred, nor lessened by any doubt, nor by any temptation from the devil, who finds no entrance into the kingdom of peace. This is the peace of which we may have a foretaste, in this world, if we have accustomed ourselves to look upon God as our Father. And yet, strange as it may seem, even when that true peace of God has taken up its abode in our hearts, we still retain a deep and abiding sorrow for our sins. Our attitude in the sight of our heavenly Father is that of penitent, prodigal children, who love much because much has been forgiven them. We can, and we do heartily join the penitent David, and say: "Have mercy on me, O God, according to thy great mercy. And according to the multitude of Thy tender mercies blot out my iniquity. Wash me yet more and more from my iniquity, and cleanse me from my sin. For I know my iniquity and my sin is always before me."* But this petition, to be washed yet more and more from our sins, and the fact that our sins remain before us, must not be understood to imply in us a belief that they are not forgiven. They are the sentiments by which we give expression to a penitential spirit, which, like the fear of God, must remain in us till our last

* Psalm l.

breath, but which neither disturbs our sweet peace, nor the confidence that our heavenly Father has forgiven us. On the contrary, it perfects that peace, and is, moreover, an evidence that the same comes from God. It is a participation of that peace which Jesus left to His Apostles when He said: "Peace I leave with you, My peace I give unto you. Not as the world giveth, do I give unto you. Let not your heart be troubled, nor let it be afraid."* Such is the peace enjoyed by those children of God whose views of Him are in harmony with the teachings of the Gospel.

But if we have the misfortune of seeing God principally and habitually as our Judge, then farewell to peace of conscience. For we shall fall into a state of mind so very distressing as to make life itself a torture, and one, too, bearing no slight resemblance to that which is brought about by the sting of the worm that dieth not. We shall now examine that state, in order that we may never fall into it, or that we may speedily arise from it—if we are actually suffering its well-nigh intolerable agony.

There is a certain class of pious persons who are never satisfied with their past confessions. Their sins are always before them, and as if they had committed them but yesterday. Every

* St. John xiv. 27.

time there is a retreat or a mission, a pious novena, or any special devotion, they must make a general confession, though they have already made several, and have, in all probability, been told never again to confess those sins. But they have forgotten the prudent advice, or they do not think it prudent, and they begin to prepare anew their general confession. Then, ignoring every confession they have ever made, or looking upon every one as null and void, not to say sacrilegious, and looking upon themselves as actually loaded with every sin they have ever committed, they work themselves into a state of nervous excitement and dread, which so confuses everything in their mind as to render it almost impossible to make any confession at all, in the proper spirit. In this state of mind they begin the torture of self-examination, and dig up the whole past. Every thing they have ever done is carefully called up, examined, cross-examined, and distorted into some monstrous crime—which they fear God will, perhaps, never forgive. Sins which they committed when mere children are as great and awful in their disordered imagination as those into which they fell after having attained the full use of reason. They had, it is true, confessed all these sins before as well as they could, but then they had no contrition; so at least, they imagine. Even now, they fear they have no contrition; for they do not feel it as they desire. They, therefore, dread that their sins will not be forgiven—even after all the mental torture through which they are now passing. The confessor, with much difficulty, seems at last to succeed in making them believe in God's infinite mercy, and finally gives them absolution in His Name. They go, apparently satisfied, but in less than half an hour, they are back in the confessional, to explain again and again sins which they have repeatedly, and more than sufficiently, explained; and also to express again their fears that there is no mercy for them.

Is not this a sad state of mind? It is not only sad, it is simply horrible. It reminds us, even in spite of ourselves, of the reprobates who clearly see that their repeated sins, and their impenitent death, have made it impossible for the mercy of God ever to reach them. By their perseverance to the last in sin, they have made themselves hopelessly and irrevocably the property of God's enemy; they are for ever excommunicated from the Heart of God, without one ray of hope. They are, in consequence, filled with a despair and a wretchedness which eye hath not seen, nor ear heard, nor heart of man ever been able to conceive. It is, as it were, a shadow of those intolerable sufferings which they endure, who have allowed doubts of God's goodness and mercy to find place in their minds. And what is the cause of it all? A partial cause may be the imprudence of those who allow, or advise, or even require such persons to make general confessions; but, if well examined, the principal cause will be found in wrong views of God. In their eyes, God is only a Judge, and not a Father. He is the God of infinite purity; the Holy of Holies, before Whom the very angels are not pure. He is the thrice-holy God, Who abominates every sin, and Who punishes even an idle word with terrific severity. The natural consequence of this one-sided view of God is the state just described—a state of mind the most deplorable that can be imagined, leading not unfrequently to insanity.

Quite recently, a most estimable and pious person ended her life by taking poison. She had become possessed with the belief that there was no mercy for her. She made many general confessions in order to obtain peace; but they seemed only to increase instead of curing the evil, and she eventually became hopelessly insane. She was placed in an asylum where every attention was bestowed upon her, but all to no purpose. Having found means of escaping, she procured poison, and ended her life. Is it not sad to see a once pious lady, and mother of a family, closing her days in such a manner? True, these extreme cases are not of frequent occurrence. But even if this were the only case, it is certainly tragic enough to show to what sad consequences wrong views of God may lead those who entertain them, and persist in them.

Now, Christian soul, are you one of those whose misfortune it is to be always tortured about their past sins? Can you be numbered among those who are always fearing their sins are not forgiven, and who are ever desiring to make general confessions? If so, it is best to tell you that, in all probability, you will never find by oft-repeated general confessions, the peace you so ardently desire.

The sacrament of penance was instituted, it is true, for the express purpose of establishing peace between God and man. It is, therefore, the great and abiding fountain of peace, which in His infinite mercy and compassion, God has left in His Church. But it must, as every other gift of God, be used in the proper manner, and in the right spirit; otherwise it may be perverted, as any other blessing, into an occasion of positive harm. Now, it is so perverted by these useless, ill-advised general confessions, which rather disturb the soul than give the peace which is so ardently sought.

God alone is the source of peace. "Grace unto you," says St. Paul, "and peace from God our Father, and from the Lord Jesus Christ. Blessed be the God and Father of our Lord Jesus Christ, the Father of mercies, and the God of all consolation, Who comforteth us in all our tribulation."* All true and lasting consolation and peace come from God, as the light and heat come from the sun. They are His own gifts which He bestows upon all who make a proper use of the means which He has appointed. But your groundless anxieties and repeated general confessions are not such means, especially when you have been told by a prudent confessor never to mention or explain your sins any more. This certainly cannot be pleasing to God, and, therefore, cannot incline Him to give you that peace of conscience which is the result of a filial confidence in His infinite mercy and goodness.

It is evident, from all that has been said in the foregoing chapters, that one of the most efficacious means to obtain this confidence is to look upon God as your Father. See Him, therefore, as our Blessed Lord represents Him pressing His prodigal son to His bosom, forgiving him all his misdeeds, giving him the kiss of peace, and, in the joy of His heart, calling

* 2 Cor. i. 2.

upon the angels to rejoice with Him at the return of His wandering child. Here is a true picture of God your heavenly Father: for it is drawn by the hand of Him Who is "the Way, the Truth, and the Life." Seeing Him in this light will not only fill you with unbounded confidence in His mercy, but will, moreover, induce Him to bestow upon you that peace which He alone can give. You will soon find it easy to trust that your sins are forgiven. And the remembrance of them, instead of filling you with alarm and gloom, as heretofore, will fill your heart with a most tender love for your heavenly Father, Who, by an act of unspeakable clemency, has not only blotted them out, but has, moreover, restored to you all the rights and privileges of children, which you had lost by your sins.

Another means to obtain peace of conscience is, to make frequent and fervent acts of confidence in the mercy of God. These acts have a wonderful efficacy, because they reach the very Heart of God, and peace flows from it, not unfrequently, at the very moment the act is made. Say, for instance: O my God and Father, relying upon Thy infinite goodness and promises, I humbly, yet confidently, trust that Thou hast forgiven me my many sins; that Thou hast washed me in the precious blood of

Jesus Christ, Thy well-beloved Son; and that however unworthy I may have been of so great a favour, Thou hast made me Thy child again and clothed me anew with the robe of innocence, and restored to me all the rights which I had lost by my sins. Such acts as these, made in all simplicity, will obtain for you abundant peace, for they open the Heart of God, while repeated general confessions, which manifest a want of confidence, rather close it.

It is evident, then, that looking upon God as our Father fills us with perfect confidence in His infinite mercy and eventually gives us peace of conscience. It does more. The thought that God is really our loving Father is a very sun, under whose rays our souls receive the warmth and health which enable them to grow in strength and perfection; while narrow-minded views of God, which represent Him almost exclusively as a terrible Judge, prevent their rapid growth, and even introduce in them dangerous diseases. Let us give a little illustration.

Suppose you place a plant in a hot-house, and then paint all the glass red, so as to exclude every other element of light except this red colour; what will be the inevitable consequence? Your plant will soon lose its freshness and health. In that red glare it will be stunted in growth; it will bear only a few sickly blossoms, little or no fruit, and will be in danger of perishing altogether. No care or attention of yours can ever restore it. You may water it, dig around its roots, prune it—all will be useless. Nothing but the whole light of the sun, which contains, besides the red, all other colours, blended into the one life-giving white light, can ever restore this plant to health and vigour, or cause it to bloom and bear its fruits in abundance.

This illustration speaks for itself. It is a striking image of those persons who shut out of their souls almost every attribute of God, except the severity of His justice in punishing them. In the awful glare of this exclusive attribute, they lose their freshness and vigour; their spiritual growth is stunted; their virtues sicken, scarcely bloom, and bear no fruit. No care of their own or of their directors can restore them. There is but one remedy, and that is to admit all the attributes of God into their soul: His infinite love for us, His mercy, His tenderness —in a word, His fatherly character. In this life-giving light they will soon revive, recover their health, and grow rapidly in every virtue. For this looking upon God as our Father is not only a sun that warms and invigorates, it is, moreover, as the gentle showers which nourish and strengthen us to weather the storms to be met with in the spiritual life. They who habitually view God in that light will surely enjoy the blessing spoken by the prophet: "Blessed be the man that trusteth in the Lord, and the Lord shall be his confidence. And he shall be as a tree that is planted by the waters, that spreadeth out its roots toward moisture: and it shall not fear when the heat cometh. And the leaf thereof shall be green, and in the time of drought it shall not be solicitous, neither shall it cease at any time to bring forth fruit."*

In closing this chapter, I must remark, for fear of being misunderstood, that, in all I have said about general confessions, I did not mean to condemn them as useless or dangerous. I only spoke of the abuse of them. They are good, and God makes use of them, at times, to bestow a lasting peace on souls that had for a long time been in darkness and trouble. They are good to increase humility, or for other purposes not prompted by scrupulosities or ill-grounded apprehensions; and we know that saints have practised them. It might then be asked: when shall I know that the motive inducing me to make a general confession is a good one, and ought to be

* Jerem. xvii.

accepted as such? The infallible rule is to listen to the voice of a wise director, and never to deviate from it, notwithstanding any doubt or anxiety to the contrary. This humble submission will make you a true child of God: "And your heart shall rejoice; and your joy no man shall take from you."*

* St. John xvi. 22.

accepted as such? The infallible rule is to listen to the voice of a wise director and never to deviate from it, notwithstanding any doubt or anxiety to the contrary. This humble submission will make you a true child of God: "And your heart shall rejoice, and your joy no man shall take from you."

* St. John xvi. 22.

, as
com-
ants to

ed of those
timately con-
a perfect right
reator, and their
ey totally depend
inued preservation,
ave, or can have, either
r of grace. Being their

CHAPTER IX.
VIEWING GOD AS OUR FATHER PRODUCES PERFECT LOVE.

WE shall now endeavour to see that looking upon God in the light of a Father is one of the means whereby we reach the perfection of love, which all who are leading pious lives so ardently desire. Before entering upon the subject, however, I must remark, that in all I am to say about the love of God, I do not mean that sensible love which most pious people enjoy, when they first give themselves to God; for, although even this sensible love is very often enjoyed by those who habitually view God as their Father, still, as it is in nowise essential to perfect love, there is no reference to it whatever in this chapter.

All who serve God, in this world, are impelled to do so by four distinct motives, or principles. These are, fear, duty, the love of God, and the hope of a reward hereafter. We shall speak here only of those motives which have a distinct reference to God. In some persons the three motives of fear, duty, and love, seem to blend and harmonize so completely that no one of them predominates over the others; while, on the contrary, there are other persons in whom one of these motives so predominates as, in reality, to become the main spring of all their actions. Hence, all who serve God may be divided into three general classes. This division, however, has no reference to their state of life, but only to the spirit in which they serve God. For, whether they be married or single, secular or religious, their service of God takes its character from the motive which is predominant in their minds.

1. The first class is made up of those who habitually view God in the light of a terrible Judge. The most prominent and striking feature which they see in Him is an appalling justice and severity in punishing sin. These serve God principally from a motive of fear, as did the Jews: and their service may be compared to that which is given by servants to their master.

2. The second class is composed of those who, in their meditations, have intimately convinced themselves that God has a perfect right to their service. He is their Creator, and their Sovereign Lord, on Whom they totally depend for their existence, their continued preservation, and for whatever they have, or can have, either in the order of nature or of grace. Being their

Lord, in the fullest possible sense of the word He has a perfect right to command them, and they feel themselves bound to obey Him in all things. This being their view of God, they serve Him willingly, and even cheerfully, from a principle of duty. Their service of God is very much like that which is given to a powerful monarch by his loyal subjects.

3. The third class consists of those who view God as their Father and their Redeemer, as the God Whose tender mercies are above all His works, as the God of love. They see in Him so much goodness, mercy, compassion, beauty, and so many other amiable perfections, that they love Him with a generous, joyful heart. Hence, their service of Him is like that which is given by good children to an affectionate parent. It is evidently the most perfect service possible, and the only one which God commands and desires under the New Law: "Thou shalt love the Lord thy God, with thy whole heart, and with thy whole soul, and with thy whole mind. This is the greatest and the first commandment."*

But you must not infer from this that the other motives are not good. They are most certainly good, because they are supernatural, and they, moreover, contain love. For among

St. Matt. xxii. 37.

those who are living piously and aiming at Christian perfection, it is impossible to conceive of one serving God exclusively from a fear of hell, or purely from a principle of duty, without any love at all. The mere fact of their leading good lives is in itself evidence of their love. "He that hath my commandments and keepeth them, he it is that loveth me," says our Blessed Lord. Nevertheless, love is the great motive insisted upon in the Gospel—not only because it is by far the most perfect in itself, but also because it implies both fear and duty, over which, however, it largely predominates.

Love implies fear, because the fear of God being a gift of the Holy Ghost, it must dwell in us as long as we live in mortal flesh. Hence, the fear of God, which is the beginning of wisdom, and the charity of God which is poured forth in our hearts by the Holy Spirit, must ever dwell inseparably in our hearts, during our earthly pilgrimage. Love also contains the principle of duty; for he who serves God principally from a motive of love, sees as well as any one, if not better, that it is our bounden duty to serve God, because He is our Creator and Sovereign Lord. But He sees far more. He beholds God in a light which makes Him appear lovely beyond the power of words to express. The natural consequence is, that while fear and duty exercise their legitimate influence upon his mind, the love of God so completely predominates as to become the main spring of all his actions. A little reflection will make this evident.

We are so constituted by nature, that our views and ideas of men, whether true or false, exercise a wonderful influence over our feelings, affections, and conduct toward them. Our idea of a man does not change him, or make him what we may imagine him to be, but it may, and not unfrequently does, change us completely in his regard. The unfavourable opinion we have formed of another, inevitably leads us to despise, and even to hate him, while he may, in reality be deserving of our sincerest love. Suppose for instance, that you have heard evil reports about a man who, for a long time, was your bosom friend. He has pried into your private matters, betrayed your secrets, plotted against your interests, and has otherwise acted very dishonourably toward you. These reports are all false, for they are the work of base slanderers; nevertheless, they are so well chained together, and have such an appearance of truth, that you are betrayed into believing them as firmly as if they had been proved in a court of justice. Now, what is the consequence? Undoubtedly it is that you now despise, and even hate, this former friend, unless you are a Christian and know how to forgive. But even then your tender love for him is gone. You are totally changed in his regard, and will remain so until you discover that all the charges brought against him are false.

This being a well-known law of our nature, we find it manifesting itself in the same manner in reference to God. Our idea of God—whether true or false, or one-sided—evidently does not change Him; but it may and does change our disposition toward Him, for better or worse. The fact is, that our views of God, true or false, exercise over our whole spiritual life an influence which it is difficult to exaggerate. Moreover, they inevitably lead us to exercise an influence over others—always in accordance with our own peculiar views of God. This is especially the case, if we happen to be directors of souls, pastors, superiors in religious communities, parents, teachers, or in any other way clothed with authority to teach our fellow creatures.

From all this, it is evident that, if our idea of God has been drawn almost exclusively from the Old Testament, we shall habitually look upon Him as our Sovereign Lord, Judge, and Master. The natural consequence is, that the fear, and even the dread, of God will predominate in us. We may be faithful servants, and even loyal subjects; but we shall never have the feelings of children toward God. On the other hand, it is equally evident, that if we have drawn our ideas of God from the Gospel, we shall behold Him in the light of a tender Father, and our love for Him will be in keeping with the character in which we see Him. It will be spontaneous, ardent, and filial. Let us attempt, if it be possible, to make this still more evident by a brief illustration.

In the days of chivalry, there was a young soldier who served his King with great devotion. He was brave, impetuous, and devoted. On one occasion, while fighting gallantly under the very eyes of his Sovereign, he received a severe wound, which compelled him to abandon the field. The King, who loved him much on account of his bravery and devotedness, wished to be present while the wound was being dressed. No sooner was the young soldier's bosom uncovered than the King cried out in a transport of joy: "My son! my son! It is my well-beloved son!" And so it was. By certain marks, he recognized a son, whom, while yet an infant, he had lost in an insurrection, twenty years before.

Were I now to tell you that this discovery had no effect whatever on the young soldier's mind; that it did not not awaken a new thought, or feeling, or emotion, or a love different from what he cherished before, you would say that such a thing is utterly impossible. You would maintain, that in discovering a father in the good King, however much he may have loved him before, a new fountain of love broke forth in his bosom, and that a tenderness which he had never felt, now flooded his soul. You would persist in saying that he had new thoughts, new feelings, new joys, and that, in the golden light of this discovery, he saw a new and glorious future dawning upon him. You would certainly be right in maintaining all this; for it is so completely in accordance with our nature that we should be filled with astonishment at finding it otherwise.

Now, this is precisely what will happen to you, if you discover a Father in God. So wonderful will be the change in your whole interior that you will seem to yourself another person—living in another world. New, and great, and sublime thoughts of God will crowd upon you, and a joy "which surpasseth all understanding" will take up its abode in your heart. All that inordinate fear of God which had brought so much distress and darkness to your soul will be for ever banished, and love, a true filial love, will become your predominant motive for serving God.

But, besides looking upon God as your Father, you must also habitually consider yourself as His child. No doubt, you will immediately say: What is the use of insisting upon this? If God is my Father, is it not evident that I am His child? So it is; and it must be confessed that, at first sight, what I wish here to insist upon appears useless. Yet, when we come to look at it practically, we find it a very difficult thing; because it involves the firm belief that God loves each one of us personally and that, too, with unspeakable love. It is all very easily said, but, nevertheless, a most difficult thing for us to believe and to realize. The fact is, that very few persons can be persuaded, and very few can persuade themselves, that God really loves them as He is said to do. They dare not believe it. They may believe it; yea, feel certain of it, in the case of others whom they look upon as very holy. But they can scarcely believe that it is so with themselves, because they are in their own eyes, so selfish, imperfect, and unamiable. It is very probable that even the saints never could realize, in this world, the immensity of God's love for them. It is related in the life of St. Elizabeth, of Hungary, that her director found it quite difficult to convince her that God loved her more than she loved Him.

You see, then, that it is far from useless to insist that we should always view ourselves as children of God. For it is the realization of this great and consoling truth which will eventually make us believe that God loves each one of us personally, and which will infuse into our soul a peace and joy which the world can neither give nor take away. If you now examine yourself for a moment, you will probably discover that you have never looked upon yourself personally and distinctly as God's child, and that such is far from being the light in which you consider yourself even now. Let us see. Do you firmly believe that God actually loves you not merely in the mass, as a member of the human family, but personally and individually? Are you persuaded that, at this very moment, God is actually loving you with an infinite love? Do you believe that He is now looking upon you with greater complacency than ever earthly father and mother felt when gazing on their first born? Do you believe that God's love for you is greater, by far, than that which either father or mother, or any other creature ever had for you? Most probably you do not. You would, perhaps, be afraid to believe that so great a love is actually overshadowing you. And yet nothing can be more certain. The love of parents is but of yesterday; it is as imperfect, as finite as they themselves; while the love of God for you is from eternity, and will last unto all eternity—if you continue to love and serve Him unto the end. All human love, however intense, is less than a drop in the ocean when compared with the immensity of that which your heavenly Father has for you. "For God is charity. By this hath the charity of God appeared toward us, because God hath sent His only-begotten Son into this world that we may live by Him. In this is charity; not as though we had loved God, but because He hath first loved us, and sent His Son to be a propitiation for our sins."* This certainly is love incomprehensible, for which eternity itself will not seem long enough to thank our heavenly Father. And this brings us to the last reflection I wish to lay before you.

The view of God, as our Father, which has been the subject of this little book, is not the only one taught in the Gospel. There we see that God is also our loving Redeemer, Who having clothed Himself in our weak nature and become flesh of our flesh, and bone of our bone, suffered most terrible tortures, and submitted to humiliations so deep that no human mind can ever fathom their depths. "He humbled Himself, becoming obedient unto

* 1 St. John iv.

death: even the death of the cross."* Can any greater love be conceived? He had said a few moments before His Passion: "Greater love than this no man hath, that a man lay down his life for his friends."† But He laid it down amidst the greatest sufferings, not only for His friends, but even for His enemies.

It was from this wonderful manifestation of Divine love, as from an inexhaustible fountain, that the saints and martyrs drew that love which enabled them to live such holy lives, and to suffer so much. And it is to this same source that we, too, must go, if we desire to see our love for God increased and made perfect. If we meditate often and seriously upon the life, the sufferings and ignominious death of a God made Man, and realize, as we shall, the fact that He "hath loved us, and washed us from our sins, in His own blood,"‡ our love will soon know no bounds. We shall find ourselves able to say with St. Paul: "Who, then, shall separate us from the love of Christ? Shall tribulation? or distress? or famine? or nakedness? or persecution? or the sword? .. But in all these things we overcome because of Him that hath loved us. For I am sure that neither death, nor life, nor angels, nor principalities, nor powers, nor things present, nor things to come,

* Phil. ii. 8.   † St. John xv. 13.   ‡ Apoc. i. 5.

nor might, nor height, nor depth, nor any other creature shall be able to separate us from the love of God, which is in Christ Jesus, our Lord."*

Such is the love that shall be kindled in our hearts, if, besides looking upon God as our Father, we also view Him habitually as our loving Redeemer.

In conclusion, let me exhort you Christian soul, to think often upon God as your Father and Redeemer. Pray often and fervently that in future, the idea of Father and Redeemer may always accompany the thought of God, and be for ever inseparable from it. Then, indeed, the thought of God, instead of bringing dread and gloomy forebodings to your soul, will ever be the source of peace and joy. It will become the very sunshine of your life, as well as your strength and confidence at the hour of death. Yes, when your earthly pilgrimage draws to a close, and the sorrows of death begin to encompass you, the remembrance that God is your Father will enable you to be sweetly resigned to His holy will. And the additional thought that the Judge before Whom you are to appear is none other than your Saviour, Jesus Christ, will fill you with unbounded confidence in His mercy and compassion.

* Rom. viii.

GOD OUR FATHER.

One of the unspeakable condescensions of our heavenly Father is the fact that He hath given all judgment to His Son. "For neither doth the Father judge any man: but hath given all judgment to the Son. . . . And He hath given Him power to do judgment, because He is the Son of Man."* O most consoling thought! We shall be judged by Jesus Christ as Man. It was as man that He suffered and died; and it is as man also that He shall sit "with great power and majesty" to judge the living and the dead. Having lived as man in this world, and experienced all the sinless infirmities of our nature, we may rest assured that He knows what allowance is to be made for the infirmity of our nature. For, as St. Paul tells us, "We have not a High Priest who cannot have compassion on our infirmities: but one tempted in all things as we are, without sin."†

. The thought of appearing before such a Judge will not only banish from your bosom any inordinate fear, but will also fill you with unbounded confidence in His infinite mercy and compassion. It will, moreover, clothe you with a supernatural strength and courage, which will enable you to say with the prophet, "The Lord is my light and my salvation, whom shall I fear? The Lord is the protector of my life: of whom

* St. John v. 22.   † Heb. iv. 15.

shall I be afraid? . . . My enemies that troubled me, have themselves been weakened, and have fallen. If armies in camp should stand together against me, my heart shall not fear."*

In such noble and Christian sentiments of perfect resignation and confidence will you breathe your last in peace, with a well-grounded hope that your Saviour will judge you in mercy, and say to you: "Come, blessed of my Father, possess the kingdom prepared for you from the foundation of the world." Then will your heavenly Father press you to His bosom, give you the kiss of peace, and bestow upon you "the crown of life." Then will you begin to enjoy, in the company of the saints and angels, the life of heaven, which the enraptured St. Augustine thus eloquently describes:

"O life, eternal life, which God hath prepared for them that love Him; that life, the sole principle of life; happy, secure, quiet life; pure, chaste, beauteous, holy life; that life which fears no death, dreads no sorrow; life devoid of spot or stain, devoid of pain, corruption, anxiety or trouble; where there is no enemy to assault us; no sin to seduce us; no fear to intimidate us; but perfect love, one and the same spirit in all; where God is seen face to face.

"Happy mansion of glory, the desires of my

* Psalm xxvi.

heart are directed to thee. Thy infinite beauty constitutes the delight of my soul; the more I consider thee, the more I languish with love for thee; sole object of my ardent desires, I am charmed with the sweet remembrance of thee.

"There are the harmonious choirs of angels; there the assemblage of heavenly citizens; there the joyful procession of those blessed souls, who from the sad pilgrimage of this life, return to the never-ending joys of their heavenly country. There the choir of prophets, whom the spirit of God enlightened with a knowledge of future events; there the twelve first preachers of the Christian religion, the blessed Apostles; there the victorious army of innumerable martyrs; there the sacred assembly of confessors; there the true and perfect religious; there the holy women, who overcame the pleasures of the world and the infirmity of their sex; there the virgins and youths who surpassed their years by their virtues and sanctity. These all rejoice in their proper mansions; and though the degree of glory in each is different, yet the joy of all is common, and shall be so for eternity."*

Think often upon this glorious life, this never-ending happiness which the heavenly Father has prepared for His beloved children, and the thought will gradually detach your heart from

* Medit. c. xxii.

this world, and cause you to sigh for a better one. Look up to your heavenly home, where God's children are filled to overflowing with the most perfect and complete happiness, and you will feel yourself encouraged to suffer patiently, to fight manfully against all your enemies, and thus to win the "Crown of Life."

BURNS & OATES' LIST

OF PRAYER-BOOKS FOR ALL AGES,

Beautifully Printed, Bound, and Illustrated,

Forty-First Thousand.

THE PATH TO HEAVEN: the cheapest and most complete Book of Devotions for Public or Private use ever issued. Cloth, lettered, 2s.; Neatly bound, red edges, 2s. 6d.; Neatly bound, clasp and rim, 4s.; Roan, lettered, 3s.; Roan, full gilt, clasp, 4s. 6d.; French morocco, gilt edges, 4s.; Calf, red edges, 5s.; Morocco, 6s. and upwards.

Hundred and Sixtieth Thousand.

THE GARDEN OF THE SOUL: New Edition, with all the additional Devotions in general use. Cloth, 6d.; Cloth, large paper, superior, 8d.; Cloth, embossed, gilt edges, with Ordinary, 1s.; French morocco, gilt, 2s.; French morocco, rims and clasp, 3s.; Calf, 3s. 6d.; Best morocco, 4s.; Gilt, 5s.

With Epistles and Gospels. Cloth, red edges, 1s.; Cloth, clasp, 1s. 6d.; Roan, embossed, gilt edges, 1s. 6d.; French morocco, 2s.; Gilt, 2s. 6d.; Calf, 4s.; French morocco, gilt rims and bar, 4s.; Best morocco, 4s. 6d.; Gilt, 5s. 6d.; Velvet, 6s. to 21s.; Ivory, 15s.; Ivory, elegantly ornamented, 21s.

GARDEN OF THE SOUL. 18mo. Edition, good type. Cloth, 1s.; With Epistles and Gospels, roan, 1s. 4d.; With Epistles and Gospels, French morocco, 3s,; With Epistles and Gospels, calf, 4s. 6d.; With Epistles and Gospels, Morocco, 5s. 6d.

Burns and Oates' List of Prayer-Books.

GARDEN OF THE SOUL. Large type for the sick and aged. Large 18mo. [*Reprinting.*]

GOLDEN MANUAL: or Complete Guide to Catholic Devotion, Public and Private (thick or thin paper). Roan, gilt edges, 6s.; French morocco, 7s.; Calf, 8s. 6d.; Morocco, 9s. 6d.; Gilt, 11s.; With Missal complete, 6s. 6d. extra; With Epistles and Gospels, 1s. extra; Velvet, rims and clasp, very elegant, 24s.; Ivory, 15s.; Ivory, beautifully ornamented, 42s.; Morocco, antique, 21s. to 45s.

PARADISE OF THE CHRISTIAN SOUL. By Horstius. A New Edition. The only complete translation in English of the admirable and well-known "Paradisus Animæ Christianæ." Beautifully printed in a pocket size, double columns; with six beautiful engravings by J. L. Hallez (a pupil of Overbeck). Cloth, 6s.; Roan, 8s.; Calf, 10s.; Morocco, 12s.; ditto extra, 14s.

This is unquestionably the most copious Manual of Meditative Devotion extant, and is a necessary companion to such books as the "Golden Manual," and others which are more distinctively collections of prayers.

MISSAL FOR THE LAITY. Abridged Edition, 32mo. Cloth, 1s.; Roan, 1s. 6d.; French morocco, 3s. 6d.; Gilt, 4s.; Calf, 4s. 6d.; Morocco, 5s.; Gilt, 6s.; Ivory, ornamented, 12s. and 21s.

MISSAL. New and complete Pocket Missal, in Latin and English, with all the New Offices and the Proper of Ireland, Scotland, and the Jesuits (thick or thin paper). Roan, embossed, gilt edges, 5s.; French morocco, 6s. 6d.; French morocco, gilt, 7s. 6d.; Calf flexible, red edges, 8s. 6d.; Morocco, gilt edges, 9s. 6d.; Morocco, gilt, 11s.; With plates, 13s.; Morocco limp, turned-in edges, 14s.; Red and black, morocco elegant, with engravings, 30s. and upwards; Ivory, beautifully ornamented, 42s.; elegantly carved, £5 5s.; Velvet, rims and clasp, very elegant, 24s.; also an edition beautifully illuminated

Burns and Oates' List of Prayer-Books.

PRAYER BOOK OF THE ORATORY OF ST. PHILIP NERI. With Special Devotions for various Seasons, &c. Cloth, 3s. 6d.; French morocco, 4s. 6d.; Calf, 6s.; Morocco, 7s.; Morocco, gilt, 8s.

THE CHURCH MANUAL, with Epistles and Gospels. Roan, 2s.; Neatly bound, gilt edges, 3s. 6d.; Calf, 5s.; Morocco, 5s. 6d.; Gilt, 6s. 6d.; also in various elegant bindings; Ivory, elegantly ornamented, 15s. and 21s.

CATHOLIC CHILD'S GUIDE TO DEVOTION: a First Prayer Book for the Young. In large type, with engravings. Cloth, 6d.; Bound, with sixteen extra plates and hymns, 1s. 6d.; Morocco, 2s. 6d.; Gilt, 3s.

THE CATHOLIC'S VADE MECUM; or Select Prayers for Daily Use. A new and beautiful edition, with red borders, ornaments, &c. Calf, 5s. 6d.; Morocco, 6s.; Morocco, gilt, 7s.; with clasp, 2s. extra; Antique morocco, with clasp, 15s.; Antique morocco, extra gilt, 21s.; Antique morocco, tooled edges, &c., 25s.; Ivory, with rimmed clasp, 21s., 25s., and 31s. 6d.; Ivory, very elegant, 42s., 63s., and 70s.; a few copies from the original plates still on sale, cloth, 2s.

CATHOLIC'S DAILY COMPANION. Roan, 1s.; French morocco, 2s. 6d.; Gilt, 3s.; Calf, 3s. 6d.; Morocco, 4s.; Gilt, 4s. 6d.; Ivory, 12s.; Elegantly ornamented, 21s.

THE POCKET PRAYER-BOOK, with beautiful engraved borders, illustrations, red lines, &c. Cloth gilt, 3s.; Calf, 5s. 6d.; Calf, tuck, 6s.; Morocco, 6s.; Gilt, 6s. 6d.

THE LITTLE BOOK OF THE MOST HOLY CHILD JESUS. A Prayer-Book for His children. By Canon Warmoll. Second Edition. 1s.

SEPTEM: or Seven Ways of Hearing Mass. By Father Rawes. Cloth, 1s.; Boards, fine edition, 2s.; Red edges, 2s. 6d.; Calf, 4s.; Morocco, 4s. 6d.

Burns and Oates' List of Prayer-Books.

FLOWERS OF DEVOTION. Diamond type. Roan, 1s; Tuck, 1s. 6d.; French morocco, 2s. 6d.; Calf, 3s.; Morocco, 3s. 6d.; Morocco, gilt, 4s.; Morocco or Russia, in case, 9s. 6d.; Morocco, antique, photographs, and clasp, 15s.; Ivory, 8s. 6d.

KEY OF HEAVEN. Cloth, 6d.; Roan, 1s.; French morocco, gilt, 2s. 6d.; Calf, 4s.; Morocco, 4s. 6d.; Gilt, 5s. 6d.

KEY OF HEAVEN, with Epistles and Gospels. Roan, gilt edges, 1s. 6d.; French morocco, gilt, 3s.; French morocco, rims and bar, 4s. 6d.; Gilt, 5s. 6d.; Velvet, 6s. to 21s.; Ivory, 12s.; Ornamental Ivory, 21s.

CATHOLIC PIETY. Roan, 1s.; and other bindings, as above.

DAILY EXERCISE. New Edition, with beautiful engravings. Cloth, 6d.; Bound and gilt, 1s.

VITA DEVOTA. Cloth, 9d.; Roan, 2s.

MANUAL OF THE HOLY FAMILY. With the Hymns, 6d.; Strong cloth, 8d.

PRAYERS OF ST. GERTRUDE AND ST. MECHTILDE. Neat cloth, lettered, 1s. 6d.; Cheap edition, limp cloth, 1s.; French morocco, red edges, 2s.; Best calf, red edges, 4s. 6d.; Best morocco, plain, 5s.; Best morocco, gilt, 6s.

THE EXERCISES OF ST. GERTRUDE. 1s. 6d. and upwards, as above.

THE DAWN OF DAY: a Prayer-Book for Children. 1s.

MANUAL OF THE SACRED HEART. New and beautiful Edition. Cloth, 2s.; Red or gilt edges, 2s. 6d.; Calf, 5s. 6d.; Morocco, 6s. 6d.

MANUAL OF THE SACRED HEART OF OUR LADY. Same prices.

CHILD'S MASS BOOK. 1s.; Coloured, 1s. 6d.

FEW FLOWERS FROM THE GARDEN. 2s.: Calf, 3s.

BURNS & OATES, 17, PORTMAN STREET.

BOOKS PUBLISHED

BY

MESSRS. BURNS AND OATES.

———o———

THE TWO-SHILLING UNIVERSAL PRAYER-BOOK.

THE PATH TO HEAVEN;

The Cheapest and most Complete Book of Devotions for Public or Private use ever issued. (41st Thousand.)

UPWARDS OF ONE THOUSAND PAGES FOR TWO SHILLINGS.

It contains :

1. All the usual Devotions for Morning and Evening, Prayers at Mass, for Confession, Communion, the Sacraments, the Sick, &c.

2. Litanies, Novenas, Devotions, and Hymns, in regular order, *for every month in the year* (including Indulgenced Prayers), intended for use in Evening Services in Churches, as well as in private. This is an *entirely novel feature*, and will, it is presumed, make the Volume a *sine quâ non* in every Mission.

3. Offices : besides Vespers, Compline, Office of Immaculate Conception, &c., it comprises the "Bona Mors," Novena of St. Francis Xavier, and Sacred-Heart Devotions, used by the Jesuit Fathers ; the Holy-Family Devotions ; the Devotions for the Precious Blood ; also Meditations, and the EPISTLES AND GOSPELS for the Year.

4. The most copious and varied collection of *Hymns and Sacred Songs* hitherto published (293). Music, 1s.

Price:

	s.	d.		s.	d.
Cloth lettered, Two Shillings.			Morocco, gilt	7	0
Neatly bound, red edges	2	6	Morocco, gilt extra	8	0
Roan, lettered	3	0	Morocco, gilt, rim and clasp	14	0
Cloth, rims & bar, red edges	4	0	Velvet, rim and clasp	10	6
Roan, richly gilt and clasp	4	6	Best Turkey morocco	8	6
French morocco, gilt edges	4	0	Best Turkey morocco, gilt	10	0
Calf, red edges	5	0	Ivory	12	0
Best calf	7	6	Ditto, best ornamented	42	0
Morocco	6	0	Best Velvet, rim and clasp	30	0

The Imitation of the Sacred Heart. By the Rev. Fr. ARNOLD, S.J. Translated by a Father of the same Company. 12mo, 4s. 6d.; or in handsome cloth, red edges, 5s. Also, calf, 8s. 6d.; morocco, 9s. 6d.; ditto, lappets, &c., 12s.; antique morocco, illustrated, 25s.

Approved (in a letter to the Author) by Father ROOTHAN, General of the Society of Jesus, and by four Theological Censors.

"Of all the books which we have seen on this Devotion, it is at once the most solidly practical and the most fervently devotional."—*Dublin Review*.

The New Month of Mary; or the Second Eve. By the Right Rev. Bishop DECHAMPS, of Namur. Translated by the Author of the "Life of St. Theresa," &c. &c. Cloth, 3s.

A Thought for each Day of the Year. By P. MABIN DE BOYLESVE. Translated from the French by WILFRIDUS. Cloth, 2s. 6d.; calf, 5s. 6d.; morocco, 6s.

The Popular Choir Manual. A Cheap Collection of easy and attractive Catholic Music for Morning and Evening Services during the whole course of the Ecclesiastical Year. Morning, 3s. 6d.; Evening, 5s. 6d.; or in one vol. 10s. 6d.

This work carries on and completes the plan of "Webbe's Motetts" and other works of the kind, which are found inadequate to modern requirements.

Hymns for the Year, containing also Benediction and other Latin Pieces in general use. This is *the cheapest and most complete Hymn-Book ever issued*. It contains not only the favourite Hymns from the Oratory and other Catholic Hymnals, but also many new and beautiful Hymns and Sacred Songs by St. Alphonsus, &c. Price 3d. Also, very strong cloth, 5d.

HYMNS FOR THE YEAR, with PUBLIC DEVOTIONS for every Evening. 6d.

HYMNS FOR THE YEAR, bound with the VESPER-BOOK, 6d.; or in strong cloth, 1s. The most complete and cheap book of the kind.

THE MUSIC-BOOK of 244 Melodies for "Hymns for the Year," the Oratory, and all other Hymn-Books, &c. 1s.

Vocal Parts and Accompaniments to the above in

THE POPULAR HYMN AND TUNE BOOK

For one, two, three, and four Voices, with Accompaniment; containing a large variety of Hymns and Sacred Songs for general use, and for every occasion throughout the year; together with a number of Easy Melodies suited for Schools and elementary use. Edited by FREDERICK WESTLAKE, Associate of the Royal Academy of Music. One handsome volume, cloth, 10s. 6d., or in Three Parts at 3s. each.

_{*} *The style and arrangement of this Collection render it especially useful not only for public use, but also in Convent and other Schools, now that vocal music is generally made an essential part of the educational course.*

Life of the Curé d'Ars. From the French. With Preface by His Eminence Cardinal MANNING. New edition, enlarged. 4s.

The New School and College History of England. One volume, large post 8vo, 820 pp., cloth, 6s.

True Devotion to the Blessed Virgin. By the Ven. GRIGNON DE MONTFORT. Translated, with a Preface, by the Very Rev. Dr. FABER. Blue cloth, neat, 2s. 6d.

Hymns and Sacred Verses, from the Italian of St. ALPHONSUS. Neat pocket size, cloth, 1s.
N.B.—Music for these Hymns contained in the "Hymns and Melodies for the Year," 1s.

The Prayers of St. Gertrude and St. Mechtilde. Now first translated from the original Latin. Beautifully printed in a Pocket size. Neat cloth, lettered, 1s. 6d.; French morocco, red edges, 2s.; best calf, red edges, 4s. 6d.; best morocco, plain, 5s.; gilt, 6s. On thin *vellum paper* at the same prices. *Common paper* edition at 1s.

Also,

The Exercises of St. Gertrude. A companion volume, at same prices.

Fioretti; or the Flowers of St. Francis of Assisi. Translated from the Italian. Fcp. 8vo, 3s.

Sister Emmerich's Meditations on the Passion. Full edition, fcp. 8vo, cloth, 3s. 6d.

Our Lady's Dowry; or how England gained and lost that Title. A Compilation by the Rev. T. E. BRIDGETT. With 4 Illustrations by H. W. BREWER, Esq. Second edition, 9s.

St. Liguori's Preparation for Death. Correct Translation by the REDEMPTORIST FATHERS. New People's Edition. 2s.

BOOKS FOR CATHOLIC SCHOOLS.

Primer, with woodcuts. 1½d.
Book I. (woodcuts), 2d. ; Primer and Book I. together, 4d.
Book II. (woodcuts). 5d.
Supplement to Book I. (woodcuts). 4d.
Supplement to Book II. (woodcuts). 6d.
[These Two Books supply the want of additional reading which is often felt in the junior classes. They also comprise elementary lessons in writing and arithmetic.]
Book III., containing more advanced lessons. 8d.
Book IV., containing lessons for the higher classes. 1s.
The Child's Spelling and Reading Book, 6d. ; or, the Two Parts separately, 4d. each.
[By means of this Book, with its simple musical notes, and other appliances, children acquire spelling very rapidly and accurately.]
Tablet Lessons, including Alphabet and Figures, in very large type, 1s. 6d. ; Alphabet and Figure Sheet by itself, 2d.
The Pictorial Reading-Book ; many cuts. 1s. 4d.
The Catechetical Reading-Book for Schools. In Two Parts. Part I. Outlines of Sacred History and Scripture Geography. Part II. Lessons on Doctrinal and Practical Subjects, following the arrangement of the Catechism used in Schools. By the Very Rev. Canon GRIFFIN, Nottingham. Cloth, 1s. 4d.

A New Historical Catechism. Price 4d.
——————————— Chart. 2s. 6d. ; rollers, 5s. 6d.

Lessons on Christian Doctrine, on a Sheet. 2d.
Full Catechism of the Catholic Religion. By the Rev. J.
 FANDER. Limp, 1s. 6d.; cloth, 2s.
Introduction to the History of England. 1s. 8d.
History of England for Children; Plates. 3s.
History of England for Colleges and Families. 6s.
Catechism of the History of England. 6d.
Manual of Christian Doctrine. 3s.
Manual of Church History. 2s.
Reeve and Challoner's Bible History. 2s.
Prints for ditto, coloured. 16s. and 12s.
Children's Mass-Book for Singing, &c. 1½d.
Old-Testament Stories. 1s. 4d.
Gospel Stories. 1s.
Manual of Confirmation. 2d.
Robinson Crusoe (revised for Catholic Schools). 2s. 6d.
The Poetical Reader. With Marginal Notes and Biographical Notices of Authors by a Teacher. 1s. 6d.
Poetical Selections by De Vere. 8s. 6d.
Sacred Poetry for Schools. Pocket size. 1s.
A Popular History of France. Illustrated. 3s. 6d.
Pocket French Grammar. Cloth, 1s.
Vade Mecum of French Conversation. 1s.
Catechism of English Grammar. Wrapper, 2d.; cloth, 3d.

Burns' Series of New Standard Lesson-Books adapted to the Revised Code of 1871.

BOOK I. adapted to STANDARD 1, 6d.
 ,, II. ,, ,, 2, 7d.
 ,, III. ,, ,, 3, 10d.
 ,, IV. ,, ,, 4, 1s.
 ,, V. ,, ,, 5 & 6, 1s. 4d.

Primer, separately (being Part I. of Book I.), 1s. 2d. per doz.
Lesson Sheets of the same, large type, for Schools, 1s. 6d.

Daily Exercise. New edition, with new and superior engravings. Cloth, 6d.; bound and gilt, 1s.

The Consolation of the Devout Soul. By the Very Rev. JOSEPH FRASSINETTI, Prior of St. Sabina in Genoa. With an Appendix on the Holy Fear of God. Translated by GEORGIANA LADY FULLERTON. 3s. 6d.

Devotions for Country Missions, with full Collection of Hymns. 6d.

Family Prayers, from Catholic Sources, old and new. 2s.

The Spirit of St. Teresa. 2s.; red edges, with Portrait, 2s. 6d.; calf, 5s.; morocco, 5s. 6d.

Spirit of the Curé d'Ars. 2s. Also in various bindings, as "St. Teresa."

Manna of the New Covenant; Devotions for Communion. Cloth, 2s. 6d.

Manual of the Sacred Heart. New Edition, 2s.; red edges, 2s. 6d.; calf, 5s. 6d.; morocco, 6s. 6d.

A'Kempis. THE FOLLOWING OF CHRIST, in Four Books; a new Translation, beautifully printed in royal 16mo, with borders round each page, and illustrative engravings after designs by the best German artists. Cloth, 3s. 6d.; calf, 7s.; morocco, 8s. 6d.; gilt, 11s.

The same, Pocket Edition. Cloth, 1s.; bound, roan, 1s. 6d.; Fr. morocco, 2s. 6d.; calf, 4s. 6d.; morocco, 5s.; gilt, 6s.

Paradise of the Christian Soul. By HORSTIUS. A new edition. The only complete Translation in English of the admirable and well-known "Paradisus Animæ Christianæ." Beautifully printed in a pocket size, double columns, with 6 beautiful Engravings by J. L. HALLEZ (a pupil of Overbeck), cloth, 6*s.*

This is unquestionably the most copious Manual of Meditative Devotion extant, and is a necessary companion to such books as the "Golden Manual," and others which are more distinctively collections of Prayers.

Spiritual Combat; a new and careful Translation. 18mo, cloth, 3*s.*; calf, 6*s.* 6*d.*; morocco, 7*s.* 6*d.*; gilt, 8*s.* 6*d.*

The same, Pocket size. Cloth, 1*s.*; Fr. morocco, 2*s.* 6*d.*; calf, neat, 4*s.* 6*d.*; morocco, 5*s.*; gilt, 6*s.*

Manual of our Lady of the Sacred Heart. 2*s.* 6*d.*

New Testament. New Pocket Edition, in beautiful type, neat cloth, 1*s.*; embossed roan, 1*s.* 6*d.*; Fr. morocco, 3*s.*; gilt, 3*s.* 6*d.*; calf, 4*s.* 6*d.*; best morocco, 5*s.*; gilt, 6*s.*

Office of the B.V.M., Latin and English. 6*d.*; roan, 1*s.*; calf, 3*s.* 6*d.*; morocco, 4*s.*

The Psalter in Latin. 1*s.* 6*d.*

Ditto in English. New edition, 2*s.*

The New Testament Narrative, in the Words of the Sacred Writers. With Notes, Chronological Tables, and Maps. Neat cloth, 2*s.*

"The compilers deserve great praise for the manner in which they have performed their task. We commend this little volume as well and carefully printed, and as furnishing its readers, moreover, with a great amount of useful information in the tables inserted at the end."—*Month.*
"It is at once clear, complete, and beautiful."—*Catholic Opinion.*

BURNS & OATES, 17, 18 Portman-street, W.

www.ingramcontent.com/pod-product-compliance
Lightning Source LLC
Chambersburg PA
CBHW022133160426
43197CB00009B/1260